D0498251

Growing Up White

A Veteran Teacher Reflects on Racism

JULIE LANDSMAN

ROWMAN & LITTLEFIELD EDUCATION.
Lanham • New York • Toronto • Plymouth, UK

Published in the United States of America
by Rowman & Littlefield Education
A Division of Rowman & Littlefield Publishers, Inc.
A wholly owned subsidary of The Rowman & Littlefield Publishing Group, Inc.
4501 Forbes Boulevard, Suite 200, Lanham, Maryland 20706
www.rowmaneducation.com

Estover Road
Plymouth PL6 7PY
United Kingdom

Copyright © 2008 by Julie Landsman

"Ceremony," from *Ceremony* by Leslie Marmon Silko, copyright © 1977 by Leslie Silko.
Used by permission of Viking Penguin, a division of Penguin Group (USA) Inc.

All rights reserved. No part of this publication may be reproduced, stored in a retrieval
system, or transmitted in any form or by any means, electronic, mechanical,
photocopying, recording, or otherwise, without the prior permission of the publisher.

British Library Cataloguing in Publication Information Available

Library of Congress Cataloging-in-Publication Data

Landsman, Julie.
    Growing up white : a veteran teacher reflects on racism / Julie Landsman.
       p. cm.
    Includes bibliographical references.
    ISBN-13: 978-1-57886-837-7 (cloth : alk. paper)
    ISBN-10: 1-57886-837-8 (cloth : alk. paper)
    ISBN-13: 978-1-57886-903-9 (electronic)
    ISBN-10: 1-57886-903-X (electronic)
    1. Discrimination in education—United States. 2. Minorities—Education—United
States. 3. Multicultural education—United States. 4. Whites—Race identity. 5. Racism.
I. Title.
    LC212.2.L36 2008
    371.82900973—dc22   2008011714

♾™ The paper used in this publication meets the minimum requirements of American
National Standard for Information Sciences—Permanence of Paper for Printed Library
Materials, ANSI/NISO Z39.48-1992.
Manufactured in the United States of America.

With deep appreciation for all those who were with me along the way: my family, my husband, my son, teachers, students, friends, and mentors.

Contents

Acknowledgments

To my readers who read the very rough draft of this book and gave me their feedback over coffee or lunch: Pam Booker, Chance Lewis, Robert Simmons, Mary Williams, and Ben Mchie. You cannot know how much your support has meant to me.

To Mary Easter who has listened to me for forty years and who has helped me puzzle it out.

To Tiffany Moore who keeps me up on the best teaching practices and supports my work every day.

To Gloria Ladsen-Billings who provides us all with her wisdom and generosity.

To my readers who keep coming to readings, workshops, and seminars and who ask the questions that inspire the next book, the next article.

To students over my lifetime: you are the reason we keep going, always.

To Bill Cottman who encouraged the poet in me.

To my father who loved jazz, my mother who listened, and my brothers and sisters who know how to provide the love.

To all who sacrificed their lives for freedom, many of whom went before me in the fight.

To my husband, Maury, whose work on this book especially made it come alive for me. Your patience is a thing of beauty.

To my son, Aaron, and his wife, Johanna, who have given me unconditional love.

To Shane Price who has been willing to have the conversations, and his patience with my mistakes.

To professor Joseph White, for his friendship and mentoring.

To Jill Breckenridge who has been there all along and helped me discover a safe space.

To the Saturday Tai Chi Group at Homewood Galleries who provide a beloved community.

To John King who encourages my work during countless morning meetings over breakfast.

To Carolyn Holbrook who understands the way life spirals around sorrow and joy.

To all those who work for social justice and equity every day—you are all our hope for a peaceful future.

Note to Reader

I want to show how my white life, from my earliest years, has informed my teaching. At times I have to take into account the ways being a woman has also determined perceptions and possibilities. There are also moments in this book when I note the financial privileges I have had and my fortune to have been born to a family with money.

Yet, I also know that one way white people attempt to minimize the effects of race is to redirect the discussion to gender, class, sexual orientation, age, physical ability, or other privileges. This allows us to avoid the uncomfortable conversations we might get into if we explored the highly charged and complex issue of race.

My goal here is *not* to avoid such an exploration. How has my experience living in my white skin—walking in it, shopping, buying a car, getting a loan, driving in certain neighborhoods, hailing a cab—impacted my life? How has it influenced the matrix of my classroom? When intersections of race with gender and class occur, I hope I bring them in without detracting from the power of whiteness.

This is one woman's journey into the space of reflective practice. If there is one thing I have learned after *A White Teacher Talks about Race* was published in 2002, it is that many students, staff, and faculty are hungry for dialogue on this topic. Many have asked me over these past years, "What is your story?" "What influenced you, what were your mistakes?" Perhaps this will help.

I have also learned that because I am white, I may be accepted and believed when I discuss skin privilege, while a person of color will be called "oversensitive," "strident," or "divisive," for making points identical to mine. This privileges whiteness, and I hope it will disappear. There is a certain irony that white privilege enables me to get this book into the world.

Some names in this book have been changed to protect privacy.

Introduction

Trying to get a white person to describe white privilege is like trying to get a fish to describe water.

—Anonymous

In my mind I do an inventory: rooms, objects, and bookshelves. I think of houses in Connecticut or whole beaches that stretch from Chilmark to Gay Head, Massachusetts. In the house where I spent the majority of my elementary school years, there were slanted roofs and hidden spaces, long hallways, and the baby grand where my father improvised his favorite jazz tunes, scotch on the sideboard dripping from neglect, ice melting into amber.

In these early years I lived in a place with a tennis court and cherry tree. Nearby, Ted, seventeen, was forcing his sister Martha, twelve, to have sex. She told me about it as we climbed in and out of the lopsided Chevrolets her brothers were working on and sat on cracked vinyl seats, breathing in the smell of plastic and apples from the orchard. The following day we would sit next to each other on the bus, ride to Center Elementary School, and go to our separate classrooms. How similar we looked to each other, with our blond hair and blue eyes, and how radically different our lives were.

Turning the prism of my life at an angle, I see chandeliers in the dining room, shining over breakfast at St. Margaret's. My privilege seems to coalesce in that school, in those dormitories, arranging itself to my advantage. In this school I absorbed assumptions of acceptance, of college plans, of entry.

Then Wheaton College in Massachusetts and finally George Washington University, 1964: here in Washington, DC, my friends, roommates, and I stayed up late to plan marches around the White House. Black, white, and Latino, we stretched out on the living room floor, beer in a cooler in the hallway, and talked about logistics and picket signs.

Where do I focus my story? Perhaps, I will jump in when I got married and lived in New Haven, Connecticut, and young black men and women came to the teen center where I supervised after-school programs. This was 1967. While most of these sixteen- to eighteen-year-olds had dropped out of school, they gave up hours of their time to create a production, one that spoke in their voices, about their problems. At the same time I was working on this play in the evenings, I ate lunch in the Gothic-style cafeteria at Yale with its lead paned windows where Maury, my husband, was in graduate school. When the young men and women at the Center asked me what my husband did, and I told them he was in graduate school at Yale, they nodded their heads, and told me they barely knew where Yale was located, even though it was only a few miles away from their neighborhood.

So often, as teachers, we see our classes as blocks of bodies, first hour humanities, fourth hour U.S. history. In our hurried work and with little time between classes, we do not have the leisure to know each student's intricate individual history. We barely have a chance to learn that Lakeesha's father is a policeman, and her mother is a professor, that Dante's brother is in prison, and his grandmother is raising him with a firm hand. We learn after Cindy has left school that she had been spending her nights in a homeless shelter across town and has finally moved into an apartment with her mother and father who work at Target. Yet they may all look similar to each other.

And, too, my body tells this story: an afternoon in DC. I am pinned to a bed, raped, knife on a table near my head. I was one of a sequence of women who become trophies of men, black or white or brown men; black or white or brown women. This part of the story is about gender.

When I come into the classroom, the boardroom, I bring body and memory. Into my school each year came those who had their own memories of trauma, disrespect, stories of shame. Somehow we managed to intersect with each other and work together. How do we, as teachers, as students, as parents manage such an intersection successfully? This is what matters to me now. Looking back on my life some lessons were repeated at each stage, only with more depth, more emphasis. These were the themes of connection, assumption, luck, and identity.

How do we separate out the parts of a stream? How do we divide up our lives into clean divisions of water?

Kevin Powell (2003) says in response to his new knowledge of women and the part he has played in their subjugation:

> This consciousness, this knowing, is a river of no return. I have finally learned how to swim. I have finally learned how to push forward. I may become tired, I may lose my breath, I may hit a rock from time to time and become cynical, but I am not going to drown this time around. (p. 67)

Knowledge about skin privilege creates Powell's "river of no return" for whites who take it in. My hope for this book is that it enables us all, through reflection and action to push forward, changing in meaningful and real ways the racism that still exists in our education system. Until we do that the American dream is not a possibility for millions of children and adults.

1

The World as Home

LESSON 1: LANGUAGE AND SONG

From my most unconscious moments I was spoken to and sung to in white dialect. I started out with whiteness bending over my bassinet in the night singing "Claire de la Lune" and "Rock a bye, Baby." I did not hear a southern drawl or a slight Italian accent, the kind my friend Guy Pucci still has.

In an essay from the book *The Skin That We Speak*, Lisa Delpit (2001) describes what happens when children learn that their mother's way of speaking, their father's way of singing, is wrong. The result is "to stamp out not only the child, but those from whom the child first received nurturance, from whom she first felt love, for whom she first smiled. There is a reason our first language is called our mother tongue" (p. 47).

I think of parents holding their babies so that music and skin become one; I wonder what happens when such beauty is designated not beautiful.

What do we do when we tear kids away from this continuum of sound and song those first moments they enter the classroom? What would happen if we used all voices and songs, as a basis for story and connection? For instance, in recognizing Ebonics as a gift, as a form of bilingualism, and celebrating this in poetry and in prose, school becomes a place where African American students are not crossing into unfamiliar territory when they enter the front door. Hearing her mother's song and speech in some context of her elementary class helps a young child make a visceral connection between the two physical locations of her life: home and school. Later, reading Langston Hughes, Zora Neale Hurston, or Tony Morrison, she will feel the connection between home and great literature, dialect and mainstream English in a more conceptual way.

It is in singing then, and in the stories my parents told, that I locate my earliest training in whiteness. I never felt a wrenching away from familiarity when I entered preschool or grade school. My mother's and father's voices, their rhythms and chants and patterns, were echoed in the patterns and sounds of safety and love I heard in the classroom.

In quick succession there were three more children born to my parents: Lesley, Mark, and Claudia. Much later would come Peter. Accompanying each baby was a ladder of song, of body rhythm, of early morning humming along with breakfast smells of coffee and oatmeal.

I understand the presence of preschools where black or Latino women or men care exclusively for black and Latino babies. It makes sense to me. Perhaps these early childhood centers geared toward one culture are successful because they provide a place where, for just a while longer, the melody, the common note following note, the expectation of breath following breath in just this pattern, is not severed from the child. Rather he or she is still at home in the world.

Reflection: In what ways was your early education difficult, jarring? In what ways was it in sync with your home culture?

Suggestions: Explore ways to create preschools where children spend part of their time with workers and teachers from their own culture. Consider ways volunteers and community workers can come to school to be with young students from their earliest years. Find songs that reflect cultures and languages and play them on a CD player each morning and afternoon as you work there.

LESSON 2: STORIES AND STORYTELLERS

My father was poor most of his childhood growing up in East St. Louis, Illinois. He was also white—a football star from Central College in Missouri where he was featured in *Ripley's Believe It or Not* for catching the most touchdown passes in the end zone in a college football game. A year later he attended Pensacola Naval flight school. In 1941 he returned from training pilots in France when Orly was a rudimentary field and planes competed with red winged blackbirds for air space. He went on to become a test pilot for Chance Vaught Aircraft. My mother was the daughter of a New England banker, product of St. Margaret's Boarding School and Connecticut College for Women. She danced in modern dance at recitals all through college, until she married and settled down. Into this family of former working class kid and debutante, I came, the first of five.

My parents often told the story of how my father brought home pilot friends for dinner on the spur of the moment. They once entertained Charles Lindbergh. Ration tickets were scarce. Much to my mother's mortification she had to serve what she considered inferior food: liver and onions.

Along with the lullabies they sang, they passed down such anecdotes. Not only the form, but the content of their stories echoed their entrée into the world of whiteness and control. I could repeat these stories of famous white people: people who were reinforced in their importance by the version of history or good literature or music my school preferred. In addition to such stories, certain words became part of my vocabulary early in my life: ski, beach, history, flight, Paris.

I absorbed early that my vocabulary, my home life was acceptable. Just as in song, in language I felt a seamless flow from front door to front door, home to school.

One key to creating congruence for all students, starting in grade school or even before, is to bring in storytellers from all cultures, to name respected people of color from medicine and civil rights, early on. And to use words from the place where students live, where their parents work in addition to those words from neighborhoods where the language of the culture of power is spoken.

Teachers are doing this all the time in our cities. Library workers and community workers, educational assistants and mentors are bridging vocabulary differences and bringing in their own stories, side by side with others who teach, who administer our schools. These vibrant places are where success is happening now.

Reflection: What stories did your parents tell you? What words did you learn or absorb that you used in school in your early years? Did your vocabulary from home prepare you for school? Did your teachers speak the way you spoke?

Suggestions: Find heroes of all kinds. I have seen preschool teachers talk about heroes to kids as young as three years old, describing in simple terms their greatness, their accomplishments. Use picture books that are in Spanish or Hmong, Somali or Russian whenever possible, showing all students stories from many cultures and the similarities across these cultures.

LESSON 3: TRUST

One of my earliest memories is being separated from my mother by the cream-colored bars of a crib. I was two years old, lying in the hospital where I was to have my tonsils removed. There is a scrim over my vision here, a gauzy screen that is at once beautiful and terrifying. She is above me for a moment, and then a single light takes her place and comes toward me. I lose everything afterward, cannot remember the ice cream they fed me, the pampering that must have accompanied my days along with the pain and the quick healing of a child raised with fur lined coats and the smell of Chanel Number 5.

My mother said that this memory was real and described how hard it was to leave me, to give me over to the doctors. She must have sung to me, later, in the house with the pine paneled study. She must have been big with her second child, my sister Lesley.

My father must have hovered somewhere in the background. In all the pictures from this time, they hold me with great confidence. Their eyes deliver the message that this is the way life is supposed to go, all is proceeding according to plan.

Do the parents of even the youngest in our classrooms have a similar confidence? Even my father, who did not grow up with money, raised me to trust the doctors, teachers, and legal system to treat me with fairness.

Some African American friends say that when they were as young as four or five, they were warned about their appearance and how to behave when they were around white people. Held tightly, they were told how to speak or how to remain silent, how to look, how to avoid being hurt.

So early then, this *second sight* that DuBois (1903) talks about in *The Souls of Black Folk*, this being the observed and the observer, is being taught:

After the Egyptian and Indian, the Greek and Roman, the Teuton and Mongolian, the Negro is a sort of seventh son, born with a veil, and gifted with second-sight in this American world—a world which yields him no true self-consciousness, but only lets him see himself through the revelation of the other world. It is a peculiar sensation, this double-consciousness, this sense of always looking at one's self through the eyes of others, of measuring one's soul by the tape of a world that looks on in amused contempt and pity. One ever feels his two-ness—an American, a Negro; two souls, two thoughts, two unreconciled strivings; two warring ideals in one dark body, whose dogged strength alone keeps if from being torn asunder. (p. 4)

To be raised with whiteness was to be raised to be part of the group who defined what was human, what was norm, and, consequently, what was "other." If we are white it takes a cosmic shift to gain a new perspective.

Zora Neale Hurston captures a moment of such double consciousness in her book *Their Eyes Were Watching God* (1937):

So when we looked at de picture and everybody got pointed out there wasn't nobody left except a real dark little girl with long hair standing by Eleanor. Dat's where Ah wuz s'posed to be, but Ah couldn't recognize dat dark chile as me. So Ah ast, "where is me? Ah don't see me."

Everybody laughed, even Mr. Washburn. Miss Nellie, de Mama of de chillun who come back home after her husband dead, she pointed to de dark one and said, "Dat's you, Alphabet, don't you now yo ownself?"

Dey all uster call me Alphabet 'cause so many people had done named me different names. Ah looked at de picture a long time and seen it was mah dress and mah hair so Ah said:

"Aw, aw! Ah'm colored!"

Den dey all laughed read hard. But before Ah seen de picture Ah thought Ah waz just like de rest. (p. 9)

I am not sure when children realize they are black, but I do know I never learned I was "white" in a sense of being "raced" until I was in my forties. I may have felt my whiteness, but it was not until I read Peggy McIntosh's article "White Privilege: Unpacking My Invisible Knapsack" that I began to define it, to identify what it meant.

One morning, in a conversation with Shane Price, head of the African American Men Project in Minneapolis, I mentioned something called "Minnesota nice." I described it as a behavior typical of Minnesotans who did not want to have discussions that might be heated or bring about controversy. I elaborated on it as avoidance of conflict, in contrast to the in-your-face New Yorkers with whom I had grown up and gone to college. Shane smiled. He turned to me and said that he was from Minnesota and he was not like that, and that what I had done was to define Minnesota as white, assuming a *white* Minnesotan norm as being the way that many whites behave. He was right. All his life he had been seen as an exception to some Minnesota white norm.

After school one afternoon, about two months into the year at a middle school in Minneapolis, six African American boys were hanging around my room, waiting for the activity bus.

"Hey Landsman! Why so many white men people wear them tight pants 'stead of baggies?

"Wait, man. You see all them dudes comin' outta high schools in Robbinsdale, Bloomington? All them white kids wearin' baggies cause they copyin' us!"

"I think we gotta go preppy next and see if they do that too!"

The ease with which students refer to whiteness is sometimes unnerving, or surprising in its effect. And yet it is also a sign of trust. If they are willing to talk about white people in front of a white teacher as well as a teacher who is similar in culture or skin color to their own, it often means you have arrived at a place of trust with them. Once you have reached this point with students, a new openness happens and the world relaxes somewhat around all of you.

One day a few years ago, after a particularly open, intimate reading of their own work, a silence fell around the table of students in a writing class I was teaching. Most of the students were African American or Latino(a). We had read around in a circle about the topic "forgiveness." We felt joy, anger, and gratitude in quick succession as we heard angry letters to fathers or mothers in prison, songs of gratitude for parents working two jobs, and poems of wistful hope that things might change. In the silence, as these stories echoed around us, one boy looked up and said, "It feels like church in here. Yeah. It do. It feels like my grandma's church."

Perhaps it is in these safe places that we provide as teachers that the necessary trust is built to get on with the job of teaching. And from this we can counter even the deepest differences between us. Teachers do it constantly, by listening, by letting students' voices and stories play center stage in their rooms: morning circle time, after-school poetry clubs, book groups, and ten-minute warm ups at the beginning of the hour. The teacher who was in this particular class where I was a visiting writer had worked hard to build such trust and it was paying off. Students were writing, learning, and actually beginning to believe they might go on to graduate, perhaps even go to college.

Reflection: When were you told you were white, black, brown skinned? When did you become aware you were part of a broader culture? How did your parents or relatives explain it to you? How do you react to being called white if you are white, black if you are black?

Suggestions: Build in time for discussions of culture and even race at an early age. Accept that your students may see you as "other" for a while. Be patient.

LESSON 4: PHYSICAL SAFETY

When I was very young, I experienced great independence as a physical being. This is one aspect of my early life for which I am eternally grateful. My parents encouraged all of us to explore the land outside our rooms: the backyard with its hot slide, the driveway with its graveled stones. When I was three I rode a tricycle down to the end of the block alone and watched the blue herons on their delicate legs, balanced there at dusk, just before autumn.

My parents did not fear for our safety as we disappeared from view, did not worry about our reception down the street. The verbs of my being were active: swimming, walking, and moving. Much of my emotional strength came from this early physical safety. Tracing back this privilege convinces me that it has enhanced my life to such a degree that I have been able to overcome trauma, fear, and anxiety because of it.

If parents cannot let their children go to the end of the block safely, what does this communicate to the children? That they cannot be trusted? That the world is a frightening place?

In his classic article on human motivation, Abraham Maslow (1943) describes a hierarchy of needs we have to satisfy. He places safety near the bottom of the list of things that are most necessary building blocks to self-actualization. Safety follows closely behind food and shelter as a necessity before going on up the hierarchy. Before we can explore concepts, abstractions, values, religion, critical thinking, change, we need to be fed and housed, and we need to feel safe. Yet many urban students do not have enough food, shelter, or safety. At the same time we expect them to climb over this hurdle and go on. The least we can do is make our schools safe spaces where food is provided, where kids have time to move, climb, explore, and to learn with their body what I learned as a child: autonomy, confidence.

Reflection: What were you encouraged to do physically at a young age? What are your students encouraged to do? Are there differences between your own children and your students in their expectations and instructions about safety?

Suggestions: Explore setting up a breakfast program if there is not one in your building. Ask students themselves, perhaps in a questionnaire, about the places where they feel safe, where they don't feel safe. Advocate for as much physically active time as possible for all students, no matter what grade you teach.

LESSON 5: COMMUNITY

I learned never to speak unless spoken to. I was taught to love color in cut glass bottles in a window, to wear black velvet dresses with white collars. Yet my childhood was one without a community of elders. I had few places to turn when things were not going well at home, no aunts who would step in, or a firm gathering of relatives or family who would drop over unexpectedly, sit around the kitchen, tell stories.

When my son Aaron was six months old I left him with my mother-in-law at a picnic while Maury and I went off to be with young cousins, to joke, have a few beers, shoot some baskets, and talk about politics. I came back hours later to find him three-quarters of the way around the circle of elders, the grandparents of the Snyder tribe. His great-grandfather was there too, nodding to his children, his babies, his generation. Aaron was asleep on Sylvia's lap, ice cream visible on his little undershirt. She held him as she talked of dinners and hard work at the hair salon where she took appointments. And while all these people had white skins, they also had a cultural heritage of struggle and discrimination, of religious persecution in their not too distant past. Along with its sorrows, its horrors, this family, this group, this community, this "cousins club" had a cohesiveness I never experienced in my own extended family.

In my family, if we had left Aaron with a gathering of relatives, he would have been gently laid down on a bed of blankets and kept in another room or put in a playpen. Does this make sense, this difference? Was it Maury's Jewish family that made his experience different? Was it the constant presence of a community, his "cousins club" on Sundays, his acceptance into the clan unconditionally, as a child with big ears and pudgy build that made him different from me? I am not sure how much of this we negotiate is related to culture, how much is connected to each individual family practices.

I do know that with all the beauty and continuity I experienced in my earliest years, came an insistence on being an "individual" at an early age. As a child, even in the midst of great good faith, this manifested itself as a lack of warmth. My parents' love sometimes felt conditional, dependent on my correct behavior, appropriate silence, good grades, and good posture. I am quite sure my parents did not mean to give me the message that there were conditions on their love or acceptance. Yet somehow it felt that way. I believe we lose a bond with the world when we are raised to concentrate on ourselves as individuals. We lose the colors, songs, and dances of the entire human family. And this begins so early, the way our babies are presented to the morning, the evening.

When schools take into account the strengths of culture—be it the communal strength of some and the individual motivation of others—students get to experience a multifaceted way of viewing the world. When schools create global connections from a very young age, in music, paintings, pictures, languages, and stories, all students become comfortable. These schools encourage students to work in groups or families. In building a more communal approach to the school day, students quickly feel secure in many contexts. They feel a part of a mixture of school and street, store, and neighborhood. They experience a congruence between all parts of their world.

Looking back I am aware that race did come into my life at a subconscious level through music, through the constant sound of my father playing trumpet and piano. My father sang along when Perry Como, Louis Armstrong, Nat King Cole, Bing Crosby came on the radio: a rich mixture of black and white pop. I did not see these singers and thus did not know the visible fact of their skin color. We did not have a television until I was seven. Yet I was aware of something different in the voices, the accents of Lena Horne, Ella Fitzgerald, or Sarah Vaughn from those of Patty Paige or Peggy Lee. Music made its home in my dreams. When he could not sleep, Dad played trumpet while I drifted asleep after story time.

This love of jazz and blues from an early time has served me well. It has always been a way for me to learn about students, their parents, their communities, how we work together. Through music and art, through theater and performance, I have experienced beauty in so many forms. And it was groups who brought these forms to me, performing in literal harmony with each other. Music was my model for community.

In the same way, sports are effective with many young people, both white and black. Coaches today will tell you that they are able to bring a team together because they have a goal, a common driving and motivating aim beyond just individual victory. Whether it be a play, a concert, a game, or an exhibit of sculpture, we can create experiences that unite our students while allowing them to explore their individuality, their identity.

In schools nearby to where I live I have seen whole walls made into murals, courtyards or alleys turned into communal gardens. Students are learning early the power of cooperation, the way to accomplish a concrete task, reach a goal, together.

Reflection: How important was family to you growing up? How important was it for you to do well as an individual in competition with others? What did you do in groups? Did you identify as part of any ethnic group? Geographical?

Suggestions: Create building-wide group projects. In secondary schools, and even middle schools, organize students to survey the communities and neighborhoods to find out what the needs are, where there might be a garden planted, a small park created, a lot cleaned up. Become comfortable with noise and activity as students work together. Have faith in them to get the job done while being social.

2

Bridging the Divide

And what color is this flocking people? She's forgotten even to gauge. She never steps out into a public place without carefully averaging the color around her, the measure of her relative safety.

—Richard Powers, The Time of Our Singing

LESSON 6: SEPARATE WORLDS

All the while I had been living in the flow of white New England another life had been going on. All the while I ate and slept and watched a new baby sister arrive and was pushed to stores and school, brown and black people were doing the same things in their own worlds, their own neighborhoods. They only intersected my world in ways of service or subordination.

While many things have changed since I was young, many things have remained the same. There are city schools in St. Paul, Minneapolis, Chicago, New York where 99 percent of the teaching staff come from neighborhoods and suburbs that are entirely different from the ones their students live in. I once conducted a year-round staff development training for a St. Paul middle school where 90 percent of the middle class faculty came from the suburbs and were white and 89 percent of the students, many of whom were poor, lived in the city and were Latino, Hmong, or African American. There are consequences for this mismatch. And this mismatch begins early in our upbringing.

My initial knowledge of those with brown or with black skin started in Dallas, Texas, from 1948 to 1950. We lived in a new, hot, and dusty suburb. We had moved from Connecticut so my father could continue his job as a test pilot for Chance Vaught Aircraft. He desired the skies, the risk, even while they had more babies and even while my mother would continue to yearn for the broken Connecticut hillside, her ocean view.

It was in Dallas that a woman with honey-colored skin took care of us when my parents, still part of the dancing, dining, velvet set, went out to parties. This woman used to draw pictures in pencil and leave them for me by my bed. The next morning I would wake to find them there, not tracings but sketches of the things I loved: a doll on a rocking chair, my favorite hat on the bureau.

In the warm light of the bedroom she sits next to me and reads. I connect this warmth and safety with her presence. Yet I do not know her name. No matter how hard I try and call back that scene, the crisp linen of sheets, the quilt pure white with pink roses, my nightgown of soft cotton, I cannot call back her name. I believe my father used her full name with "Mrs." in front. She was older than he was and perhaps that is why. Later he would call black housekeepers by their first names regardless of age. Is it possible he became more dug in, more resistant as he grew into his forties? My mother always used first names.

I carried this dynamic from my earliest connections to people of color and to people who were poor in my unconscious with me into the classrooms, the places where I have worked or lived. And these early experiences were all the more powerful because I lived in such physical isolation from the place where those who took care of me lived. This woman who read to me, sang to me, was in a position of subordination to my parents in some manner I could not have verbalized at the time. They were her boss, drove her to and from our home when the buses ran late, complained if she did not arrive on time the evenings she insisted she could come on her own. From the earliest years of my life race and class were intertwined. She was not only a different skin color from me, but she was not even able to buy a car, like my parents could.

It has taken me my entire life to understand and to watch out for the unconscious and erroneous assumptions I learned from those early days: that black people were always poor, that we never lived near them, that there was a good reason for this.

Joseph White and James Henry Cones III, coauthors of *Black Man Emerging* (1999), help us address race in three ways. They insist we read, contemplate, attend conferences, and begin to approach our personal history and knowledge on a *conceptual level.*

Next, White and Cones say, we must engage in ongoing *dialogue* around issues of race, coming back again and again if need be, until we work things out. This dialogue is a lifelong process, in faculty meetings, at district board meetings, and in our day-to-day interactions.

A third way they suggest we experience race and culture is to *go to a place where we are not in the majority,* to a black church if we are white, to a mosque if we are Jewish or Christian, for example, and participate in a service or event together with those in the neighborhood. It is important to go to a place of discomfort in some way, to feel what it might be like to live our lives in a culture, a way of being, that is not our own, and where we may be regarded with distrust initially, even with suspicion.

All of these actions come into play when addressing the unconscious, the ritual ways we grew up.

Reflection: How separate is your life from those with a different skin color or from those of a different economic class? What position did your parents have in relation to white people, people of color as you were growing up? What did you absorb from this? How has it played out in your teaching? What status do people of color hold in your building compared to white people?

Suggestions: In the next month or two engage in all three categories of interaction that White and Cones speak about: conceptual, conversational, and experiential. Find ways to do this with a group of individuals you do not know well, or are not necessarily comfortable with.

LESSON 7: GENERALIZATION

In Dallas a black woman came to clean our house after my sister Claudia was born. I believe her name was Jean. And what is odd to me now is that I actually remember her skin color as different from the woman who used to put me to bed. Jean was darker. And just as I remember her name and her darkness I also remember her thinness. She had sculpted facial bones creating multiple shades of brown or red highlights when the Texas sunshine fell on her body, her head, as she watched us from her chair in that dusty yard.

All the while she worked in the kitchen, loading bottles into the sterilizer, and all the while she washed and made lunches for Lesley and me to take out onto the screened porch, she kept to herself something hard and sad. I am not sure I sensed this at the moment or learned about it later, when she came into my breakfast corner of yellow and green tiled light. Her head was almost bald, her face swollen with purple bruises around her jaw and eyes.

Here are the events I know from my parents and what I occasionally saw: Her husband beat her. She ran away from him. He tried to find her, sometimes coming near our home, his face in windows, disappearing before the police arrived. Even when she had already left him for a new home he showed up near our door. They said one day he caught her, and tried to burn her hair off. She arrived the next morning with her head covered by a cap, which she wore until her hair began to grow in.

Did this mean that I thought all black men were violent? I don't know how racialized my thinking had become by age five. I do know I feared his anger and my father's voice on the phone, telling him that if he came near our yard again he would be caught. In that flat and dusty new suburb, in the heat of a Dallas summer, Jean came to work through all of this. And I wonder if in her courage and even in my father's rough, white-toned alliance with her, I gathered to me a sense of her strength as well as her struggle.

If I look back now, I can see that Jean was a model of endurance and resilience. I don't believe I was raised to see her this way, however. I was raised to generalize about her situation, to judge her "group" as negative because of her husband's actions. My father, very early, referred to the behavior of Negroes as a group.

In a class I taught as a writer in schools a few years ago, one fourth grade girl read a letter she had written to her mother in prison. This girl was African American and the letter was eloquent—full of news of her school life, her grandmother's strictness, her church. Yet what registered for me immediately on hearing her read the letter was that her mother was in prison.

Before me was a vibrant, resilient, and artistic young girl, with a strong caring grandmother who oversaw her care. I did not see these strengths right away. I judged her mother. I learned to place unconscious emphasis on the negative part of her life and ignored the resilience, the courage, the strength of her own power, her grandmother's dignity and persistence in bringing her up. I believe this is because I saw her, for an instant, as part of a group, a group with negative connotations.

I went to first and second grade in a public school in Dallas with a playground made of orange powdered stones. I was in Mrs. Reese's first grade class, in an all-white school in a curving suburb of the city.

The first villain I encountered, besides Jean's husband, was a white man, who was kidnapping children off our school grounds. We were told to watch out for "*any man*" in a coat who came too close. He was not described as white. If he had been black, his blackness would have been part of the description. And his actions would have called down judgment on his whole group, whereas this white man was only bad in himself. He did not reflect on me, on my whiteness.

This naming of blackness while leaving white to be understood as the norm is interwoven into my thinking and reading, speaking and seeing. By being meticulous, by creating learning spaces where even pronouns and phrases are used with care, we may begin to counter our subconscious impulses if we are white and have been raised as I have. The trick is not to become paralyzed by this.

Reflection: Did you often hear the word "white" to describe individuals? In the news? In your neighborhood or town? Are you comfortable referring to yourself as white if you are white? Try using this word "white" before each Caucasian person you refer to for one day in the way we often refer to the blackness or brownness of those who are not white. How does this feel? (See Thandeka's book *Learning to Be White* for a description of this challenge.)

Suggestions: Develop exercises or find ones already created that work directly with prejudice. Have a conversation with your students about this. Who has to represent the whole group? Who is simply an individual? Is this fair?

LESSON 8: THE COST

Thandeka, in *Learning to Be White* (1999), says we form our views of race at pivotal moments, early on, that we take in our fathers' reactions, our mothers' glances, our grandmothers' use of language and absorb them. And so in Dallas, in the tiled kitchen, I learned from Jean about race. Hours later I learned from my father about separation.

I was four. I recited the eeney-meeney-miney-moe rhyme with my sister Lesley, vying for the last chocolate chip cookie on the white, gold trimmed plate under the cool kitchen darkness of afternoon. I used the word "nigger"—as in "catch a nigger by the toe." I have described this previously in my book *A White Teacher Talks about Race*, yet it is only recently that I have come to understand that this was a crucial moment in my education in whiteness. This rhyme and its "n-word" and the way Jean took me and sat across from me while I stood and put her warm hands on my little pink knuckled ones and stared across at me with great solemnity determined much about my racial identity. I was almost encased in Jean's thighs, my knees rubbing up against her sitting knees.

"That hurts me, the nigger word, and I wish that you would not say it. It hurts people like me with brown skin, when you talk like that." (The "n-word," the word "nigger"—how do I do this here, in telling the story now, and not wanting to write it on the page?)

I nodded vigorously, up and down, up and down, my eyes filling. I was not a child who hurt people and perhaps this is also why the moment stays with me, a crystallized memory I can still feel. The combination of hurting her, and hurting her with my use of words that touched on her blackness, made the scene doubly intense. She let me go, touched me gently on the head with her hand. I wandered out onto that porch and I felt something I had not felt before. I can only think now that it was guilt, or shame.

Later, as I said goodnight to my father, I told him about the word, how I would not say it any longer because it hurt Jean. And he, home from test piloting planes that might explode or spiral or stall in still pauses over canyons, he whom I loved for his approval already, his nod of appreciation for my dresses on Sundays or my songs at night, he shrugged his shoulders, dismissed me with words like this:

"Oh, she is such a sensitive woman, that Jean. Don't worry about it. Doesn't mean a thing. Forget it, sweetie. Colored people are like that sometime."

It was then that I knew this man who would later hold the back of my bike as I began to teeter down Dallas streets, who gave me baths, rubbed me down with rough blue towels, this man who towered above everyone we knew, could be wrong. I smiled and nodded and went into my bedroom. I let him tuck me under covers and sensed him standing there for a moment, before he went back to the dining room for the dinner my mother always kept warm for him so that they could eat across from each other in candlelight, all their babies silent for just a while.

While he did this the way he always did, leaving me warm and secure, my sister Lesley's soft breathing near by, I knew something was wrong. It hurt Jean too much for this word to have been okay and for him to be right. Of course, I could not separate from him then. I thought he created houses and roads and the whole world. I kept my confusion about him secret, never speaking of it, uncertain what to do with it. Yet it has remained with me still, so that even now when I write about it I feel such aching, not only for Jean and her thin back, turning to assemble bottles for the latest Guyton baby, but for that little girl turning over in bed, falling asleep with new anxiety in her world.

Every day we experience the struggle of people both white and of color, who are asked to deny their parental upbringing, their neighborhood music, their race consciousness in order to succeed. I would never want to ask anyone to deny her parents. But sometimes disjunctions that happen in our lives may be necessary. And I know that such a disconnect, such a break with what our parents or elders say can offer a key to understanding. While sorting all this out we may be lucky enough to comprehend the complexity and confusion our white and black students bring to our rooms, our work places.

My relationship to my father fell into a pattern of call and response, challenge, separation, and return. We sparred until he died. In that kitchen in Dallas where it began, where I pulled away from him, my body separating from his warmth, was a time that stood out. Our lives are a series of such moments. How we react to similar moments over and over each time makes up the direction we will go. Our classrooms are filled with such moments resonating for us, for our students in ways neither we nor they can fully comprehend at the time.

A few years ago when I taught at Carleton College in Minnesota, I brought up this incident in talking about how I learned about race. In describing it I said the word "nigger" as this was the subject of the incident itself. One young woman was upset. She was of mixed race, African American and white. She stayed after class to express her hurt. With her permission I started the next class off with our exchange and opened up the discussion around my use of the word and her hurt. In this class there were eight students of color and ten white students. There was no uniformity of response, either from the white students or those who were African American and Latino. Some said they had no problem with my speaking the word aloud, others said it made them uncomfortable.

Discussion around this word went on for the entire term, outside of class, in Black House, in an all-school meeting. It was the beginning of a rich, complex dialogue and demonstrated to me and others on campus that language, that what we learn and how we use it even now, is powerful and crucial to our understanding across all boundaries.

Reflection: Were there ever moments you sensed your upbringing about race was wrong? Hurtful? Have you ever found yourself separating from your relatives or friends or colleagues over the topic of race? How did you learn the meaning of racial epithets?

Suggestions: Find allies in your work place who support your antiracism curricular concerns. Meet with them as often as you can. Talk with colleagues, administrators about a clear understanding of how the school will deal with racial slurs and epithets. Be ready to have conversations when events around race come up in the news.

LESSON 9: HOPE

After three years my mother declared her desire to leave Texas, to be near the ocean. I wonder if this yearning for place is also in our muscle, in our blood: she yearned for the smells, the salt and expanse of the broken land, the sound of an August rainstorm, and the gentle breaking water on the Atlantic shore. My mother was a strong woman. She grew up without a mother, hers dying when she was only two. Her great-aunt and her older banker brothers raised her after her father died when she was twelve. And yet, being away from the place she loved seemed harder on her than anything I can remember.

I wonder what it means for the parents of immigrant children to live in a place foreign in contour of hill, quality of warmth, color, and wind from where they were last year, the year before. Even this affects our teaching, the displacement of our kids and their parents.

My father, too, was not able to imagine living in Texas forever. So, on a gamble they moved back to Connecticut before he found his next job. Along with us, came the grand piano, the china and silverware, the muted colors and manners of good little girls. Along with us came the belief in our future as solid, expected in its good news.

To this day I still believe, somewhere hidden and deep, that all will be well. From this simple belief and security came much of my ability to negotiate the world. I had constant infusions of hope. This gift from my parents, simply as a product of their own advantages as upper middle class white people in

America in the 1950s, created my resilience, my underlying belief in my own power and possibility. My race, my whiteness was never mentioned, much less as an obstacle to success.

This difference from the outlook of many of the students with whom I have worked is profound. Often, when I go into classrooms around the country, and these rooms are in schools in neighborhoods with high poverty or crime or in poor rural areas of the country, students look at me, and ask,

"Look around, lady. What do you think is going to happen to me? Look where I live, what happens to my parents, my sisters."

The most effective educators of any race or culture refuse to accept defeat. They bring a constant infusion of hope into the classroom. In a high school for students for whom the system had failed, and who were trying to catch up on credits in order to graduate, I watched teachers mention college with great consistency, saying to a young poet that his latest work might convert into a good college essay, or to a student working hard in math that he might start looking at the SAT books to get ready for that test. And while many students would brush this off, I believe it stuck with them.

The overlay of hopelessness in these young people turned out to be thin, much thinner than it appeared. Demanding college prep work, even in this school for "losers" as the students called themselves, implied that they would be going on to postsecondary education—something they never dared to dream of. This expectation, reiterated over and over, pierced the despair in many of these students until it dissolved.

Reflection: What were you expected to do in education as a child? What was planned for you and when did you become aware of this? Where did you get your hope?

Suggestions: From first grade on, work the idea of high school and beyond into the conversations in your classrooms. Imply that all your students will have choices about this. Create chances for students to visit college campuses, to feel themselves physically *present* in a college environment.

LESSON 10: SECURITY

In Milford, Connecticut, in that space of dark wood and saltwater, I thrived as any girl would who walked to her school bus along the seawall. It was a beautiful sight I saw each morning, ocean glittering in winter, white caps curling over the gray expanse of water under spring rain. Our rental house was tied together. The furniture tilted inexplicably on shortened legs, and the stuffing stuck out around exposed springs on the chairs. In the bitter damp of January that year, rain showers ran out of the ceiling and onto breakfast.

I was assured then that this was a temporary life, that our real life would begin soon, in a big country house with a place for plants on the windowsill over the sink, and where my mother would choose African violets for just this spot. Milford was an aberration, an odd year.

Too many students, in urban, rural, and suburban schools, do not have this kind of security. Whether because of homelessness or job transience, eviction or financial disaster, many children come to us wondering where they will be staying next week, next month, next year. The chance to live in one community, with heat and food and beauty, was one I absorbed without realizing it.

When we pare our lives down to their basic economic expectations and assumptions—what we have or do not have in our background that allows us to connect with students—we discover what we need to explore in order to teach. I believe those teachers who have grown up in poverty are crucial in helping me understand the lives of some of my students who live in poverty. I believe that black educators, too often dismissed by white teachers, have unique insights in understanding some of the issues of black students. Of course, there is an infinity of black teachers, each of whom have a different approach, and teachers who have experienced poverty teach in many different ways. Yet when these teachers do venture to talk about their experiences of race or poverty they are too often discounted just as women have been discounted when they bring up concerns about gender or sexual harassment.

Why are these practitioners discounted? It might be the discomfort we feel with the subject of race itself. It could also be our desire *not to know* that keeps us from responding. Because to know, to accept that there are ways we can address culture or race or class in our teaching, means we might have to change. And in addition to that we may have to question the very perspective on which we base our view of the world.

There are whole schools that thrive because they hear their staff, their teachers, their community, and their students each year. They shift curriculum, try out new pedagogies, put kids into groups more often, perhaps. Or they may hold meetings with parents to find out what their concerns are, what they want for their children. At these schools, those with experience of race or poverty or harassment or those who simply have a way of looking at teaching in a unique way are heard.

Reflection: How secure was your childhood? Did you live in a secure and safe home while you were growing up? How has that influenced your world outlook? Your view of your students?

Suggestions: Seek out teachers who are succeeding with kids you are having difficulty with. Often the expertise in working with students of all kinds is right in your building. Find the time to observe these teachers.

If you have classes where students come and go within a year, try and tailor your instruction for them. Create self-contained lessons so new students can jump right in. Put together a packet that helps kids catch up when they come to your room. Suggest someone start a student support group for students new to your school. This group can meet for five sessions, helping students adjust to their new environment.

LESSON 11: GUILT

By February of our first year back in Connecticut, my father had a good job with a company that made bombsights for airplanes. When these same bombsights were used in the Viet Nam war this would haunt me. Then it was only where he went each day when he left us. He had decided with the birth of his fourth child that he could not take the risk of testing airplanes any longer.

It is here that I want to address feelings of guilt and hence paralysis: we are not responsible for our past, for our parents' lack of insight, for their racism or the way they brought us up. It is what we do now that matters. It is how we respond to new knowledge or our own reactions or to comments that matters. It is how we go on with our lives that matters.

Guilt is a way to center the problem in ourselves, to claim attention for our sense of shame. We can get so caught up in this shame that we cease to focus on the world around us. We can miss reasons for whole families' homelessness or the effects of the closing of public spaces, libraries, parks, and what this might mean for our students and their families. In guilt we get to turn inward and stay there.

The finest white or middle or upper class teachers I have observed over the years have acknowledged to themselves and others the unfair educational advantages they might have had and then gone on. They teach, do community work, connect with their students. Gradually their defensiveness lessens, their mistakes meld into the way life is in their everyday school experience.

Reflections: Do you feel guilt over your own advantages? Does it keep you silent or afraid to ask questions?

Suggestions: Begin to ask your students, their parents, your colleagues about their lives, their hopes. Survey students and parents each fall about what they want out of this year in your class in your specific subject.

LESSON 12: VISIBILITY

At six and seven years old, I was oblivious to what was missing in my life. And it seems to me that in what was *not* there, I find my own blindness to history, perspective. Perhaps this is why such work is so difficult. It is a matter of trying to construct a world that we were absent from and that was often absent from us.

A man named Harry T. Moore, NAACP secretary in Florida, was killed along with his wife in a bombing in 1951. I did not know this at the time but learn it now. Did African Americans I did not see or talk to know this? Was it talked about in kitchens long after the kids were asleep? What did Harry T. Moore look like and was his picture on the front page of the *New York Times* and how do we mark the lives of daily heroes?

And all this time I had never heard of Jews either. I never heard stories that Maury, my husband, and his cousins remember hearing when their parents thought they were asleep. These were about the death camps and the escapes and the deaths and the fear and the relief and the gas chambers and the showers and the piles of bones and the stripes and the skeletons behind barbed wire. Sometimes tears accompanied these stories and a recitation of names of those gone. Here were narratives told around dining room tables not far from my home. Yet this was never part of the ongoing story of the world I lived in.

African American students at a predominately black high school in North Minneapolis were moved and astounded to learn that many Jewish people alive today were denied the opportunity to work on the yearbook, the school paper, or to join the debating team because of their Jewishness when they were younger and went to the same high school. Listening to these stories as part of a history project that required them to interview past members of their community, hearing of the discrimination against "white" Americans, opened the students' eyes to a broader relationship with injustice.

The absence of information goes so many ways. It seems to me the great gift of our schools is to fill in these absences for students.

Once when I mentioned to an audience that I did not know about the contributions of the Buffalo Soldiers in the westward expansion in this country, the place of the black cowboy in its settlement, a woman raised her hand. She said that I should also know that the Buffalo Soldiers went along with the genocide of Native Peoples in their incursion into the West. She said this is a part of the story as well.

It is in making mistakes or omissions that I learn the most valuable information. From her I learned that one story leads to another, one perspective to another, resulting in more and more understanding of the whole picture. And if students get a chance to experience a new turn in the spiral of knowledge as they grow, this in itself is a great achievement. It is the kind of critical thinking and learning that standardized tests often cannot measure.

In a family movie of that first year by the sea, my father is standing on the seawall. He is holding Claudia, the newest baby, in his arms and the rest of us are next to him imitating his every move. He twirls around holding out his coat with one hand, Claudia tucked under his arm with the other. We twirl with him, in perfect unison. He stops and bows. We stop and bow. He is in suede. We are in red wool shirts and corduroy trousers. He smiles as he moves, one foot out, we move, one foot out. We are in sync. My mother is somewhere behind the camera, near the house facing the ocean.

It was one of the whitest years I would ever live. I entered school surrounded by the image of white women teachers, librarians, and nurses and this made things feel in white sync, between school and home.

And in this year too I was taken places—New York, Boston—and the ease with which I went there, created in me an assumption of welcome into the broader world. Mary Easter, an African American friend raised at this same time, told me of her father, a professor at a black college, taking her to New York from Virginia and being turned away from a hotel in Manhattan where he had a reseveration. This was the first time he had not planned to stay in Harlem. Even with confirmation in hand, his wife and daughter by his side, they told him he was not allowed. I must have been staying at these same hotels at just this time.

Never once in these years did I witness an indignity to my parents. Never once was I denied entry.

Reflection: What do you know about now, that you were oblivious to as a child? From whose perspective did you learn of current events, history, literature?

Suggestions: Develop critical thinking skills in your students. Create units, subjects, topics, themes from many perspectives. Find materials that ask students, even young ones, to imagine and understand about perspectives not their own. Talk about the principles of Kwanzaa at an all-white school, the Native American perspective on Columbus's arrival at a diverse middle school.

3

Discovering Omissions, Countering Isolation

LESSON 13: STRUCTURE

One late August morning in 1956 my father took three of his children down
to Stonewall Pond. This saltwater cove connected to the bay near Menemsha
Harbor in Martha's Vineyard and on out to the Atlantic. I was thirteen, my sister Lesley was eleven and my brother Mark was nine. We were there to watch
Mark take his first solo sail on our sailfish. Clouds rolled in as Dad shoved the
flat-boarded boat and my blue-lipped brother alone onto the pond. As Lesley
and I stood on shore, we could see swells of white and black green water build
higher with each gust. Mark crouched over the rudder while he pushed in the
centerboard. He held the sheet clamped in his teeth, as he was taught to do.

A sudden fist of wind caught the sail, spun it flat, and the boat went over.
Mark emerged from under it, leaned on the centerboard, brought it up,
grabbed the sheet, and reached for the rudder as before. He went over again.
And again. Dad paced the shore, while out on the water huddled one blue
shiver of a kid, leaning his spindly body on the centerboard time after time.

I stood nearby wrapped in a towel. I asked Dad to let us row out and bring
him and the boat in. I was sure Mark's arms would give out. Dad knotted his
jaw in a telltale sign of fury and kept walking back and forth as rain started
falling and cabin cruisers pushed in to moor at places throughout the cove. Finally, Lesley and I sat down on wet sand and covered our faces with our towels, peeking out only once in a while.

He went over, struggled up, and went over again. I lost count at twelve. Finally, I heard a motor, and a rough voice call back toward our huddled figures, our straight-backed father. I looked through spread fingers to see one of the native Islanders, a year-round fisherman, heading out in his dingy. He loaded my brother into his boat. He let down the sails of the sailfish, gathered them in and towed the fish behind him. Mark sat in a huge raincoat, shaking so hard his bones seemed disconnected, face buried in the yellow lined hood. When they arrived on shore, Dad walked silently to the edge of the beach, pulled in the fish, tied it to the mooring post and rolled up the sails. He slung them over his shoulder and walked toward the car, rudder and centerboard in his other hand. Les and I took off our towels, wrapped Mark in them, and thanked the man who stood, holding the spare rain coat, shaking his head:

"Crazy son-of-a-bitch summer people."

In the car, on the way home, I could see my father's face in the rearview mirror. He kept glancing back toward where his son sat. Mark pulled his arms toward himself, held his body tight under towels, tried to find warmth there. The rudder and centerboard clattered in the back of the station wagon. No one said a word for hours after we got home. Then Mark, after a tense dinner, mused from deep in his wool sweater, as he sat by the fire, "How long you think he would have left me out there?"

This scene was one of the first times I sensed that our father's need for control was greater than his ability to understand a situation and that this need could be dangerous.

I know many teachers who insist on control. They insist on it in definitions of history, of good, of bad. They insist on using the same authors over and over when they teach because they feel in control of the content.

Some talk in the halls about how angry they are when children cannot speak English well enough to be understood and to respond to demands. Any situation that feels out of their control calls up more rigidity.

I do not confuse structure and limit setting with control. Students need structure—a predictable arrangement of class guidelines and order—to be able to learn and to feel they are in a safe place to speak and work. They need to see the teacher in charge. Many of my black colleagues have been telling me this all along, insisting that white teachers, often white female teachers, are too timid or afraid in this regard, not willing to spell out clearly and firmly what is expected.

It is a balancing act, this need for structure, for concrete instructions, while at the same time being willing to abandon total control when the students veer into a direction that might yield important dialogue. All of us, white and black, struggle with when to step in, when to hold back.

There was also an assumption of power on my father's part in the sailing incident: a lack of appreciation or respect for the working class man, who saved his son. My father communicated to us in many ways that we could *assume* respect from others. When this did not happen, we could ignore those who disrespected us, as he did Mr. Mayhew. Often as teachers we assume respect as a given. Over and over, I have learned from colleagues and my students that this assumption is not valid. As much as we may not want to believe it, some black students may not automatically respect and trust their white teachers as readily as they may respect and trust their black, Latino, Native, or Asian teachers. We may have to earn their respect and this may take some time.

In one high school in Minneapolis a white teacher mentioned to her black friend and colleague that she felt this was the case, that her black students trusted her colleague more quickly than they trusted their white teachers. Her colleague thought this could not be true, that if you were a good teacher the students felt this immediately and gave you respect on the spot. Yet she mulled over this and finally one day asked her students. They verified the white teacher's observation. They said it was easier to trust a black teacher if you are a black student. "They know where you are coming from," her students said. She was surprised. Her white colleague, who had little trouble earning the respect of her black students in a few weeks, smiled. For her it was not a matter of liking this fact or agreeing with it. It was simply the case.

After I retired from regular public school teaching about eight years ago, I was a visiting writer at Work Opportunity Center, the alternative high school for students who had dropped out of their home school. I had been a teacher in this school the year before. One day a new student, Karen, walked in the door. I asked students to write on the topic "I wish" to get them warmed up for the workshop. Karen glared at me. Because I was in my fourth week visiting, the other students and I had developed a relationship, and they began to write. Finally Karen scribbled furiously in her new notebook. When it came time for her to read in the circle of readers, she read something like this:

"I wish white people would not come into my life thinking they need to know all about me before they even meet me. I wish white teachers who think they know about my life and my struggles would not assume I am going to tell them everything and write on some funky old topic like 'I wish.' I wish white people would leave me alone."

The process in this class was to have absolutely no comment after each person read. Later we might talk to someone who read something in their piece that resonated for us, but in the circle, immediately after reading aloud, no one was to make a comment. The teacher wanted to jump in after Karen read, but I signaled her to remain quiet. Karen's voice was heard as part of this circle, no more, no less. The students had grown to respect not only their teacher but also me and the setup and structure for this read-around. In the next round, Karen, realizing she truly could write about what she wanted, wrote a very powerful piece about her eighth birthday, about her father missing it because he was falsely arrested, about her birthdays since then. The next week she came early to writing class and stayed late.

I felt stung when Karen read that first piece. Yet I had to trust the process. I had to call on my faith that she would find her voice, that we would build a relationship. To *assume* trust so early was unrealistic. To let that get in the way of teaching and expectations would be a disservice.

So often students who are black, middle class, and attend schools in suburban districts where they are in a small minority experience racism in their neighborhoods, stores, streets. When they try and describe these incidents, they are often ignored or even disbelieved. I have talked to these young men and women, and even small children in elementary grades about what it is like to try and tell their stories. The toughest part of all is when teachers or students "don't believe what happened to you," say many of them.

These are students who dress conservatively, have two parent homes, and whose parents are often professionals. Yet they are stopped when driving home by police who believe they have stolen cars. They are followed around stores, while their white friends wander freely without an escort. Sometimes teachers or counselors do not suggest college, but steer them toward vocational school even when they have grades higher than their college bound classmates.

And often, because they are young and unsure of what is going on, these students are trying to figure out for themselves if what they experience is typical for their age group or is unique for them because of their skin color.

So, today, in urban and suburban neighborhoods where wealthier blacks or Latinos come to live, white teachers who meet with me tell me they are finding they have to continually check in with others about their perceptions or assumptions. They have to listen, build trust, and puzzle it out with their students. The first step, however, is to wait for the connection, the beginning of a relationship, to happen.

Reflection: Do you assume students automatically respect you? Were there times in your life when you did not automatically respect an elder? How does it feel to be disrespected because of your skin color or have respect withheld? What can you actually control in your classroom? What is out of your control?

Suggestions: Offer a one-day-per-week, after-school, make-up time for students. Invite them into your room. This provides a time when they can talk with you about what is on their minds. Build in time to build trust and community through initial exercises at the beginning of your course. It may seem difficult to take the time to do this at first, with so much material to cover, but ultimately it will pay off in fewer behavior problems and more cooperation among students.

LESSON 14: VISCERAL LEARNING

I have a beautiful rug on my floor and plants in my windows where I live now. I love glass bowls and when I lived in Sweden for four months I found a red one with striations into pink and purple, and I bought it for very little money. I have inherited my mother's glass birds that I place in the hiding places in our brick wall. All this echoes my childhood home in Woodbridge, Connecticut, where we moved in 1952, one year after we arrived back east.

I started third grade with Mrs. Hubbell in October of that year. I was so tall I could see my shadow move at the back of the column when we lined up at recess, shortest to tallest. It was the first time I remember having a sense of my body as something I could not control.

My elementary school was filled with white kids: well-off, middle class, and poor. Some came from old, run-down houses, some from mansions. My house was somewhere in between these. Our barn garage had an apartment over it that my parents rented out. There was a tennis court and a front yard that flowed down a small hill to the street corner. In the field that surrounded our property apples dropped from their gnarled branches into long grass. The driveway twirled up and around, with lots of room for cars. My father built a split rail fence around the fields. One of my best memories is walking that fence in my bare feet, balancing on the warm wood as I teetered across the whole expanse of it.

There was a basement that contained the coal burning furnace and where rats sometimes found their way into the spaces between the foundation and the walls. One night my father and I spotted one scuttling across the kitchen. Dad immediately set up huge traps all around downstairs. The next morning he threw out three rats. There was nothing he could not fix.

All this time my mother seemed in the background. She was there, making sandwiches for friends who spent Saturdays in our yard. She was there making meals. She was a presence of gentleness, a force I did not often challenge or argue with and also did not appreciate.

My father also showed us a place in our basement where he said blacks hid out on their way to Canada, along the Underground Railroad. This was a tunnel-like cave. Women, men, and children waited behind a pile of dirt set up to look as though it was the edge of the room. They were concealed in this space. What stays with me now is the musty smell, the forbidden feel of the room. One single lightbulb dangled from the low dirt ceiling. I wonder, if during the whole time I lived there, some spirit remained of the Abolitionists who brought the runaway slaves to the door. I wonder, in my most fanciful moments, if the ghosts of women, men, and children hidden away wandered my dreams. I am not a new age person. Yet I hesitate to deny that a kind of historical energy might have existed in that place.

It seems to me that this story, told early and made real by the actual rooms and earth and place of its enactment, made the ideas and descriptions more vivid to me than any book or even a television show could do. I was able to touch and feel and breathe the air and space of the Underground Railroad experience. I was able to imagine it. I have not been able to verify the truth of this story. Yet it does not matter. What matters is the way being in that space triggered my imagination. Bringing our students into rooms, into places where events happened or into reproductions of them, make their school experience a sensual and visceral one. Be they pioneers in North America, Jews during the Holocaust in Eastern Europe, slaves on ships crossing the ocean, approximating these events or conditions helps all students grasp history in a way that cannot be matched by words on a page.

After visiting an exhibit in St. Paul that included a chance to experience the feeling of the attic where Anne Frank lived, middle school students I was teaching told me it was the best trip they had ever taken. It made all they read in her diary and all they read of history come alive. They absorbed history through skin, through walking, through kinesthetic means. What better way to learn.

There are multiple stories of the part of Minneapolis near where I live now. One is about the black jazz musicians who were not allowed to stay in hotels downtown when they came to Minneapolis, and so were put up on the north side, the black section, for the night. How inspiring for young black and white students to know the richness of this place, the house where Dizzy Gillespie stayed, the room where he did a midnight set for the residents of this part of the city. The Holocaust museum in Washington, DC, is based on the idea of following an actual person through the journey of his or her life at that precarious time in history. It involves physically walking through some scenes to find out at the end of the tour of the museum the fate of your "person."

How powerful our learning about race could be if we literally *walked students through* events, times, and places in history. Teachers in middle school especially are experts at doing this. Students at this age are all action, body, movement. I have seen mock trials, reproductions of debates, moviemaking projects, neighborhood oral histories in so many of the finest classes I observe. When students are asked about what they like best about school they often name these experiences and field trips.

Knowledge comes, as we have seen and known, from our skin and fingers, our eyes and ears. From music and smell and touch. How amazing are those classes that enrich the depth of learning and empathy by creating situations where students learn in such a visceral way, the way I learned about the Underground Railroad. I think this is especially true about race because we learn racism in a visceral way, and the best way to unlearn it is through visceral experiences as well.

What stays with me from these years in Woodbridge is riding the bus to school with Susan Bartoli. She was a girl from the run-down farm who wore her hair in braids and had odd dresses that were too small for a growing body. She was the one whom the boys liked best because she was fearless. And she

was also "other," other than white, Protestant, and middle class. My parents
made this clear to me when she delivered fresh eggs to our house. After all Bartoli was an *Italian* name. That made her different from me, and in that difference I sensed inferiority.

Ethnicity, race, and religion became boundaries my parents insisted on as
long as they could. Jews were "kikes" and Cadillacs were "Jew canoes" until I
married Maury. In one letter from 1946 my father wrote to my mother from
California where he was testing an airplane, he said: "This place is crawling
with kikes. We could never live here. Too many Jews."

Because I learned messages about groups of people by osmosis these messages still reverberate with me. I classify, I stereotype, without even realizing it.
Thus when I work with a class of Hmong children, and they insist on working in a group, speaking Hmong with each other, I put this in my "Hmong
box," where I keep generalizations about these children. And when a young
woman, who is Hmong, comes along in middle school and wants to work on
her own instead of being assigned to a group, I am surprised, flustered perhaps, as this does not conform to my assumptions about "Hmongness," about
how "they" like to work in groups. I am the one who creates the boxes. Yet I
resent it when anyone creates a "white box."

It finally comes down to the fact that it is not an either/or situation: cultural inclusion *or* individual differences. It is both. It is my Protestant culture
with its emphasis on individual work and it is my white privilege and my father's compassion and fascination with the Civil War combined with my time
in history and the place I lived that makes me who I am. Such a mixture is ultimately mysterious.

Until he died, my father won the affection of all who worked for him and
helped him. The Jamaican nurses who tended him in the hospital when he was
critically ill with cancer told my brother that his father was "such a gentle-
man—so kind." And a Latina hospice nurse said to me, shaking her head, that
my father was such a sweet, sweet man, a saint. This is the same man who
played a game with epithets as we got older, saying half a word and watching
us rise to the bait: "That nig—," he would say, turning toward me, waiting for
my outrage.

I wonder if you can take part of your inheritance and hold it dear and truly
separate from another part of it, make the break.

Reflection: What do you remember learning about your own race, religion, culture, or skin color? Can you create specific scenes or dialogue? Make a list of all the ways your culture manifests itself in your life. How is gender treated in your religion? How are holidays celebrated? What rituals do you observe? Ask students to do this over the school year.

Suggestions: Create a visceral, tactile, or active lesson for your students at least once a month. Use interviewing as a way to understand literature, history or sociology, politics or immigration issues. Use photographs, cooking, walking, and working on active projects to get students involved.

LESSON 15: POWER

When we sold my parent's house in 1998 after my mother died, we learned there was an illegal restriction on the property. The neighborhood association had declared that no one could sell to anyone if the whole group of residents who lived "on this hill" did not approve the sale. If you looked around you realized that this meant no blacks or Latinos or Mohawk Native Americans. The years I wandered the fields and up into the woods, when I stood and waited for the bus on the corner of North Racebrook and Westward, or rode Sally Adams's horses around the hill, this was in effect. Then, as my skin burned in the sun, as I picked rhubarb out of the meadow across the street, where later I would kiss Tom Cole until my lips hurt, when I played tennis with Hotchy Rippere or Timmy Buxton, or played touch football with Bill Badgeley over at the Adamses' huge lawn, hugged him to the ground for the ball, I was living the life of the restrictive covenant.

So often we hear whites talk about the cliques of color in the lunch room, and the neighborhoods where suddenly they, whites, find themselves uncomfortable because they are not Latino or black. Implied in this is a criticism of people of color for being unwelcoming or standoffish or mistrustful. Yet there are groups of whites who have a history of forcing people of color into enclaves by use of our own power. We allowed, and still allow, realtors to "steer" clients to one part of our city to another. Landlords still find that no apartments are available when a black man asks to rent, yet an hour later show a white man a unit in the same building, saying it is ready for move-in.

It is dizzying to contemplate the power of language in all this.

While I was growing up in a white suburb, Lamar Smith was shot to death in front of the Lincoln County courthouse in Mississippi after seeking to qualify blacks to vote in 1955. George W. Lee was killed gangland style in Belzoni, Mississippi, after a week of terror during which whites vandalized blacks' property, also in 1955. Martin Luther King Jr. was beginning his boycotts, Rosa Parks sat on the bus after a long day and a life of civil rights work, and in 1956 U.S. Supreme courts were ruling for integration. Ku Klux Klansmen accused Alabama grocery-chain-store truck driver Willie Edwards, twenty-five, of having made remarks to a white woman and forced him at pistol point to jump to his death. Emmet Till was killed in 1955. At ten and eleven and twelve years old these and many more events occurred, and I don't remember ever hearing about any of them. In books that tell me what I was not told then, I find what was invisible to me.

Latino children can tell us about battles in their countries of origin, or about the historical events of their Mexican American or South American background, a different take on the Alamo, for example. African American kids can tell you at an early age about the principles of Kwanzaa, the events around Juneteenth celebrations, or events in their neighborhood years ago. They are full of information.

Once I watched a fellow teacher mention in a class on war and literature that the Japanese, when they were interned in camps in our own country, developed new and innovative ways to grow plants in the desert. They became ingenious, relegated to the dry, California wasteland, at finding ways for vegetation to prosper. Later, he continued, this knowledge would be useful for everyone. A Japanese American student came up to this teacher at the end of class to say how cool it was for him to hear this. He wanted to know more.

To teach we must literally know what we do not know, redefine what we assumed was defined. We have so often assumed that textbooks were neutral. Time after time we learn that they have a point of view, through omission as well as inaccuracy and incompleteness. Living the "restricted covenant" still, we have to be ingenious at discovering what is missing, what can enrich, what can redefine.

Reflection: How did you learn about politics, the events of the news, as you were growing up? From what point of view are history texts in your school written?

Suggestions: Take one event, in politics, history, literature, even science, and have students describe it from different points of view. Pick an event: wedding, graduation, first day of school are examples. Have students randomly assigned to write about this event from different points of view: the bride, the best man, the ninth grade sister, and so on. Discuss why each might feel quite differently from another about what is happening. Allow humor to enter this activity.

LESSON 16: OUR SUBCONSCIOUS

Those early years I shopped in New York with my mother, riding in on the train, going to FAO Schwartz to see the windows of Manhattan's most elaborate children's store. We stayed at the Algonquin Hotel, with its elegant lobby and velvet chairs, huge dining room with white tablecloths—even for breakfast. We went through the revolving door each Christmas time, dressed in identical outfits, young ladies' day out. Once, my sister Lesley became so excited by the way the door turned that she pushed it around and around until a line of men and women formed on the sidewalk wanting to come into the red plush lobby for drinks. My mother was mortified, struggled to stop her momentum. I learned to sit and sip ginger ale with a cherry, called a Shirley Temple, and keep my legs from jiggling.

Blacks were porters on trains or worked elevators with their silver handles or helped load our suitcases into carts to bring them to our room. I never experienced any nuanced connection with African Americans. I only interacted with blacks when they waited on me or cleaned the house I lived in.

When I mention such a white experience to teachers I speak with about race, many tell me this kind of life still exists today in their largely white suburbs. They speak of their students' attitudes toward blacks or Latinos that shock or disturb them. They recognize that students are bringing their parents' language and their perspectives into the classroom. And these same parents have often been raised in white enclaves themselves. The trick is to break the pattern. Teachers, principals, and counselors often say that their goal is to interfere with the cycle of stereotyping and false perception many whites and blacks have of each other. They are persistent and creative in changing and expanding their students' world.

It is 1956. I am twelve years old. I am sitting on the couch with my best friend, Janet Belmont. We are looking at *Life* magazine, and in it are pictures of women, white women, yelling at school children going into Little Rock, Arkansas, schools. One woman has her hair pinned to her head, bobby pins crisscrossed close to her skull, the same way my mom wore hers before a party. This woman's skin seems pulled tight against her facial bones, and she is screeching. She seems to have her mouth in a sneer of fury. We turn over the pages together, pausing at each one for a long while. I am saying how horrible that people would yell at children who simply wanted to go to school.

Janet turns to me, says something about understanding the white people: "I mean, but would you want *them* to come to your school?"

And I argue with her in a fumbling, inadequate way, but I argue.

We were never quite as comfortable with each other again. Yet I am sure that at other times, I let comments like hers go. I remember this moment as one time I did something right. I believe now that this response had everything to do with the power of the visual image, those large pictures in *Life*. As powerful as texts are, visual images are even more so. They can be used to build connections or to reinforce negative perceptions. They can motivate compassion. Used in the right way they can break the pattern of separation and isolation many of our students experience.

Internet clips, DVDs, even certain TV episodes can cross the boundaries. Student exchanges, teacher exchanges, are other ways to connect. I cannot imagine how much richer my life might have been if I had visited a school in downtown New Haven during my years of growing up in Woodbridge.

The same time as the events in Little Rock and the civil rights movement unfolded, my favorite book was *Gone With the Wind*. This book came highly recommended by my father and mother. It was one place I got my history, my point of view, of the South and race. Here is a passage about freed slaves from that book and reprinted in Robert Loewen's (1995) book, *Lies My Teacher Told Me:*

> The former field hands found themselves suddenly elevated to the seats of the mighty. There they conducted themselves as creatures of small intelligence might naturally be expected to do. Like monkeys or small children turned loose among treasured objects whose value is beyond their comprehension, they ran wild—either from perverse pleasure in destruction or simply because of their ignorance. (p. 144)

Loewen, a historian, follows this quote with the statement: "[I]n 1988, when the American Library Association asked library patrons to name the best book in the library, *Gone With the Wind* won an actual majority against all other books ever published" (p. 144).

I was an avid reader then. And in this book, I had burned into me that the separation and limitation, the rigid status of blacks and whites was part of the way of the natural world and that I was part of a superior group while blacks were like children, impulsive. Or, as Loewen says again: "In its core our culture tells us—tells all of us, including African Americans—that Europe's domination of the world came about because Europeans were smarter. In their core, many whites and some people of color believe this" (p. 144).

Gone With the Wind reached me in a way that other history or biographical books did not. The power of narrative has always been an important way of keeping my attention. And so, in this way the stories we assign, the literature our students read, because story is such a powerful thing, can reinforce or counter racist instincts. We are all, as human beings, prone to be influenced by story, by anecdote, by the told tale.

Leslie Marmon Silko (1977) opens her novel *Ceremony* with this verse:

> I will tell you something about stories
> [he said]
> They aren't just entertainment,
> Don't be fooled,
> They are all we have, you see,
> All we have to fight off
> Illness and death.
>
> You don't have anything
> If you don't have stories. (p. 2)

What we select for students to read can have a radical affect on what they think, and how they react. When a Native American parent is upset at her daughter's tears after being in class where the Laura Ingles Wilder books are read depicting Indians as savages, this is not a minor complaint or concern. When a young man comes to us and says he cannot stand to be in class where his classmates are reading aloud Huckleberry Finn because of the way it feels to him when the word "nigger" is repeated over and over each day, this is serious.

Many parents of color with whom I have talked over the years describe the trauma of sending their sons or daughters off on the bus, knowing that they may be treated with conscious or unconscious condescension. In nonverbal ways— frowns of disapproval, creases in the forehead, turns of the teacher's head—body language will tell their children too early they are not doing it "right," that they are not the remarkable, bright, delightful girls or boys their parents know and love. My parents did not worry about this with their children.

Reflection: Do you live in an isolated enclave in terms of race or poverty? Is this a problem for you? Have you always lived with those who are similar to you in terms of skin color? Religion? What are the advantages, disadvantages to this? What stories and books do you remember from your childhood? What effect did this have on how you thought about the world?

Suggestions: Organize exchanges with schools around a similar assignment: reading the same novel and discussing it together. Invite teachers from a school district unlike your own to develop a unit together in your subject area in secondary school, or around a theme in elementary school. Set up pen pal exchanges between students of color in different schools and arrange a final meeting or celebration after three months between the students.

Search the Internet, community centers, and libraries for stories and literature that present complexity, intelligence of characters of many kinds of cultures, races, and economic levels. Ask students to write their own narratives and stories, as often as you can, even in history class. For example, ask them to imagine the story of a young boy or girl in a certain era. Use the power of story as a way in—to literature, history, science, psychology.

LESSON 17: MESSAGES ABOUT POVERTY
I know now that my parents used my mother's inherited banker family money to put a down payment on their first house and, later, to pay for our college and even prep school. It was their cushion, their ease in the world. It kept them from the anxiety of living on the fragile edge, even as some in our still somewhat rural Connecticut neighborhood did.

This inheritance was my father's secret. This inheritance detracted from my father's claim of being a totally self-made man. He rarely mentioned it.

I do not discount my father's hard work, his fifteen hour days and commute to his job at Chance Vaught Aircraft an hour and a half away, his weariness, head bent over papers long into the night as I slept in my room above the circular driveway. Yet I believe there was a kind of historical thickness to our money. Even now, having inherited some from my parents after they have both died, I feel its comfort. I am aware that I can take some time to write, to pause in the every day, every year work world, to sit in a room and call up words to capture these experiences. All the years I taught I could take my summers off instead of adding a second job to my schedule.

How much does it matter that these words have been directed to a good end? I am not sure. I know I sometimes feel guilt over this good luck. It seems to me, at its most simplistic, a response to my own privilege has to be the recognition that the playing field has never been level for American children. A more beneficial response than guilt to the situation of inequity might be insisting on an end to tracking in gifted programs. It might be creating a foundation, as rich black friends of mine are doing, for scholarships to college for black high school students.

I see myself stretched out on my bed, twelve: I am ignoring my mother's call to dinner in the autumn twilight. My father is working late at work. I am engrossed in *Gone With the Wind*. Our good life at this time was attributed to my father's brilliance, my mother's goodwill, her working with the Scouts, volunteering in schools, and working at a center for elder citizens. I took this in, all of it. Yet I also took in Susan Bartoli's home, its sunken roof and its splintered front porch.

And at this time I remember another house in disrepair, the one of my Uncle Clayt, the farmer brother of my mother, the "unsuccessful man" of the four children in her family. Clayt had gone to war, gotten caught in the Battle of the Bulge, and come home crazy. He read Shakespeare at night in his room over the cow barn, and neglected those very animals below him, their udders stretching taut with unreleased milk.

I was always aware that my father felt sorry for this odd uncle. At the same time he respected what Clayt knew about orchards and soil, consulted him about roses, or how to put in fence posts.

It was in seeing and hearing my father's pity with a mix of respect that my condescension toward those in poverty was nurtured. For a while I saw my role as the helper: the one who might "raise up those poor kids" to a better life.

Along with this, I did not think of asking people what they actually wanted or needed. I assumed I knew that already. For a while I thought those in poverty wanted to live like I did.

This same kind of pity or condescension can trigger us to expect less of students: assuming they cannot handle tough courses, are too overwhelmed to do homework. With all their empathy and compassion for those who come to their schools each morning after sleeping in homeless shelters, the finest teachers demand from them what they would want teachers to ask from their own children. Not to do so is a way of giving up on them. While they may find ways to cut a deal with these students around dates due, books lost, lack of proper supplies, or for lack of computer access, such allowances do not result in lowered expectations.

I watched a fine teacher in a middle school where I was doing teacher training insist that his students go down to the cafeteria in the morning and get breakfast. He did this in such a way as to include all his students without singling out any for this requirement. He also asked students to stay after school to complete an assignment some afternoons. He knew that some of their homes were full of people coming and going. In doing this he was still expecting the assignment to be done or attention to be paid in class.

Kids sense pity and are uncomfortable with it. They also know compassion and they appreciate this. Again this is tricky work, trying to provide without making students feel conspicuous or the subject of teasing because of their home situation. It requires subtlety, nuance, and a lot of "nagging," something my parents gave me.

Reflection: Did you grow up with a lot of money? How did this affect you? If you did not have money, what did you need from those around you? What helped, what hindered you? How would your life have been different if you had had money?

Suggestion: Think of ways to make it possible for poor kids to learn: computer access, after-school homework hours, breakfast programs, supplies for students who don't have them, cell phones for homeless families. Become an advocate for one of these ideas.

4

Negotiating Power and Identity

It is, in fine, the atmosphere of the land, the thought and feeling, the thousand and one little actions which go to make up life. In any community or nation it is these little things which are most elusive to the grasp and yet most essential at any clear conception of the group life taken as a whole.

—*W. E. B. DuBois, The Souls of Black Folk*

LESSON 18: CONTENT AND STYLE

At St. Margaret's I would continue to learn the "most elusive little things." When I went back to visit my boarding school recently, I noticed how it matched my memory in its landscape, its beauty. The back patio still stretched along the entire width of the building with its glorious wisteria. The pond stood silent where swans glided, and the grounds sloped toward open land and sports fields where we played lacrosse and field hockey. As I looked out on the tennis courts and science building forty-two years after I graduated from this school, I wondered at my metamorphosis from a white girl in a blue tunic running down the side of the lawn, playing wing in field hockey, to this woman, still white yet more knowledgeable.

What I inherited, especially in that place with its dark wood and velvet, its Episcopal Church services, was a quintessential knowledge of upper class life in America at a certain time in history. Whiteness was all around me, in the books I read, in the people I met, the teachers and preachers and workers I saw.

I received instructions there: not about the world of whites or about skin color as Janie in *Their Eyes Were Watching God* did. My instructions were about being a woman, instructions about my body:

Stand up straight, tuck your stomach in, shoulders back.
Don't kiss on the first date or he will think you are easy.
Chew with you mouth closed.
Don't dance too close.
No loud colored clothes.
Wear your skirts four inches below your knees.
When eating out, start with the silverware from the outside and work in toward your plate.
Don't pull soup toward you, push it away, and then angle the spoon just enough to fill it.
Don't smoke or chew gum—you will "look cheap, like any girl from the flats."
When you go to a party, have on drink and nurse it along the entire evening. There is nothing worse than a drunk woman.
Don't wear skirts too tight, heels too high, lipstick too dark. Don't chew gum loudly or crack it in someone's ear.
Don't have sex before you are married; everyone will know if you have had it by the way you walk.
Don't appear too smart, you will lose your man.
Marry someone like you, preferably a Yale man.

I absorbed this list the way I absorbed how to sit quietly through Thanksgiving dinner with Aunt Claire in her darkened dining room.

African American students at Work Opportunity Center where I taught for a year had their own version of this list:

Don't eat on the streets, it is rude.
Don't be alone in a room with valuable equipment or jewelry, they might think you stole it if it is gone.
Don't speak the way you do at home. Speak like white people do.
Don't assume people trust or like you if they are white.
Fight for your rights. You may not get them if you don't.
Don't assume you will get the job even if you pass the tests. Sometimes they find ways to keep you out.

When you shop, keep your hands outside your pockets so no one thinks you came to steal something.

Given their own set of instructions from home students may approach us with confidence or wariness, anger or excitement. Add to this their developmental age, their desire to challenge or conform, and we have a complicated, exhilarating mix when they become adolescents.

In high school I lived in rooms of books, libraries, and texts. I was taught to read here, to truly read. I was asked to understand the sufferings of Job in Archibald McLeish's play, *J.B.*, a class I will never forget because it taught me the pain of injustice that is without explanation or reason.

I was taught by teachers who demanded that I take time to think, to mull over and over again those things I did not understand, to ask questions in class, to study five hours a day outside of class. In this secluded place, with its class sizes of twelve to fifteen students, its enforced sleep times and homework times, I learned both psychological and intellectual discipline. Today I work with students who have jobs after school, who are in classes with forty-five other students each hour, and whose families are working two jobs to keep the rent paid.

There is no comparison between my education and theirs just as there is no comparison between the education students from elite prep schools get and the education of those in high poverty high schools. Yet we expect all students to go on to institutions of higher learning and compete with each other as though they are starting from the same place. And those students from poverty schools are the lucky ones who find a way to go to college at all. Some colleges have centers where students can get extra help. Some have summer programs. All this is catch up.

I was taught to negotiate at St. Margart's: rules and bedtimes, visitors and hours with those "gentlemen callers" who came to see me on weekends. I learned Latin, French, and Shakespeare here. This was the world of "I-thought-I-was-white-until-I-met-Julie" white that a friend described when she introduced me at a reading in Minneapolis one night. This was white white.

All that danced in me emerged here, on the portico where we tried to learn the twist, moving to Fats Domino, James Brown, and Jerry Lee Lewis. Yet I rarely got to live a normal teenage life of after-school study sessions, of weekend parties. Even with all I learned about manners and deportment, about conjugating Latin verbs and thinking philosophically, there was a cost to me in this seclusion.

Many people ask me if white teachers can really connect to black children, to Native Americans or Latinos or Asians. I feel, at times, that this question hints at a cop out: a way of shrugging our shoulders and giving up. Yet I am here to say in this chapter, just in case you might think it is impossible, if I can connect as a woman with my background, then anyone who is white can connect.

For three years I lived in this place, going home once in the winter and once in the spring and then summer. And all this time, from 1959 to 1962, there were freedom riders and deaths and protests and courtroom decisions about education that would affect us all. Howard Zinn (1980), the author and historian, summarizes the knowledge I never received in his book *A People's History of the United States*:

> Still it [Brown vs. Board of Education] was a dramatic decision—and the message went around the world in 1954 that the American government had outlawed segregation. In the United States too, for those not thinking about the customary gap between word and fact, it was an exhilarating sign of change.
>
> What to others seemed rapid progress to blacks was apparently not enough. In the early 1960's they were engaging in wild insurrection in a hundred northern cities. It was all a surprise to those without that deep memory of slavery, that every day presence of humiliation, registered in the poetry, the music, the occasional outbursts of anger, the more frequent sullen silences. Part of that memory was of words uttered, laws passed, decisions made, which turned out to be meaningless. (p. 450)

All the time I studied and ate and slept in the barricaded walls of dances with Taft or Westminster, Choate or Gunnery, college students were arrested for sitting at lunch counters, others were being beaten in southern jails. Did anyone ever talk to me of these things? Never. It was only in those glorious months of July and August that I came across an accounting in *Life*, or a mention in *Time*, about the state of politics and protest. There is no doubt in my mind that I would have been much better off if I had learned what was happening in the world, in the cities, in the rural South. I would find, later, that I had a lot of catching up to do.

Many teachers have told me they don't have to teach detailed black history or literature in their schools because their students are primarily white. This is doing those students, both white and the few students of color, a terrible disservice. For all my vaunted prep school education, there was an essential, and crucial, kind of education I never received.

In visual art when I have studied perspective, I have had to take into account where I am standing when I draw a building. From close up it looms large, far away it recedes in the landscape, finally disappearing in the "vanishing point." This is a metaphor for what students need to have when they study history, literature, psychology, sociology. From the point of view of an African American or an antiracist white person or an abolitionist, the study of slavery might loom large, the presence of it might dominate the psychic landscape. To a white male or female for that matter, slavery may recede in importance, disappearing into the distance on the psychic landscape. To a union worker the study of labor history is key to his or her view of the effectiveness of laws and rights. To a manager it may not seem to matter. The best teachers bring as many perspectives as possible into play, to encourage students to see through other eyes, to note how "buildings line up" in the viewfinders of those not like them. In adolescence then, the inclusion of perspectives becomes more important, richer, more nuanced. It is one of those themes that recur over and over in teaching.

> *Reflection*: Write down a list of instructions you were given, either directly or indirectly, about behaving in the world. Look up the headlines from some of the years you were an adolescent. What was going on then? What do you remember hearing about?

> *Suggestion*: Ask students to list instructions they have been given by their parents, guardians, church group, peers. Discuss these in class and compare your list to those of your students.

LESSON 19: ADOLESCENCE

It was for my own sanity that I began to learn things, not because I would need this knowledge to survive in a hostile, mistrustful world as my black friends would tell me they did. I learned things because I was sixteen, seventeen, and eighteen and this is what you did at that age: venture outside your parents' prescribed areas and permissions.

The work of secondary teachers is as much about working with students who are pushing the boundaries of adult authority and cultural prescriptions as it is about teaching to the test. Adolescents try to make themselves visible as adolescents while at the same time feeling the pressure to blend in with their group, the crowd. It explains my own rebellion from gender strictures. It explains the immigrant female student who wants to go to the mall while her Somali parents want her to stay home to care for her siblings. We see this before us all the time in middle and high schools. We have only to dream ourselves back into our own adolescence to understand what is happening across all cultures.

I am working at a library as a volunteer "poetry lady." Most of my students are Muslim and female of all ages. They dress in hijab and come from religious homes. In their most honest moments, they speak of the frustration they feel in trying to maintain their beliefs and yet become part of the American landscape.

"I have to take care of my sisters and brothers all summer. My brothers get to play sports, hang out with their friends. It doesn't seem fair."

"I don't want to go to a Muslim charter school. I want to go to a regular high school. But I do feel safer at the charter. I don't know."

"You know we can't handle pork at all. That is why the cashiers can't put it in the bags at Target."

"My parents want me to go to college, maybe be a doctor or a lawyer. Why are so many people surprised that a Muslim family wants their daughters to do well?"

These struggles seem "old" in some historical way, a repetition of what immigrant groups have gone through before: the generational adaptation to a new country. This is the tricky territory of claiming a cultural identity while taking on a new American identity at the same time. African immigrants have a special struggle. They are often mistaken for African Americans. One Somali teacher at a high school in St. Paul told me she makes sure to speak up immediately so that people will hear her accent, and so "They will not treat me like they treat African Americans." She has observed carefully and has drawn this conclusion. This says so much.

Combine racial and cultural identity development with the hormonal changes at adolescence and you can see the tricky ground that both students and teachers in secondary schools walk each day. While I have a great respect for the need for small class sizes in the early grades, I also believe we need equally small sizes in grades seven through twelve. It has been shown that lowering the number of students in a class helps students of color and poor students more than almost anything else.

I dressed in uniformed lines for chapel, uniforms for dinner. Bells governed my days. I never experienced the night those months I was at St. Margaret's. I never spent a Saturday afternoon swimming and leaving my suit to dry on a porch railing on a warm May day. My life was as structured as a life could be.

Years later, I would compare the rules in my boarding school with the rules in the juvenile prison where many of my students had spent some of their high school years.

"Man, Landsman," they would say, shaking their heads, "you didn't even have no judge send you there? Man, your daddy sent you there! That's dog, Landsman."

I am ambivalent about this structured life. I firmly believe that order and consistency, regularity and predictability of rules and responses are good things to bring to our schools. Yet this structure also allowed for little time to explore other worlds, to hear other points of view, take risks. I was scheduled from seven in the morning until ten at night. In many ways I was stunted in my growth as an emotional human being.

Reflection: What were you allowed to do as an adolescent? Was it different from your brother? Your sister? What were your frustrations between the ages of thirteen and eighteen?

Suggestions: In every way possible try to create families or houses or learning communities that provide small groups for adolescent students. Give them time to ask questions, argue, explain their viewpoint. Become comfortable when the topic of race comes up. This is where they need to feel they can try it out.

LESSON 20: OUR BODIES, OUR VOICES

One afternoon my father drove me back to St. Margaret's after vacation. He was dressed in tennis shorts, a sweater, and the topsider shoes he wore when sailing. When he began to carry my suitcase up the stairs for me, Miss Todd, the teacher on duty that day, told him he could not go upstairs. My father asked her why. She said it was because he was in shorts, not proper for the girls to see.

A knot formed in his jaw. He simply kept walking up the steps. Miss Todd's shrill voice called to him. She said something about getting the headmistress.

He shrugged and kept going. When we got to my room he put my suitcase down, then turned and smiled, a wide smile that stayed in his eyes.

"This city boy just can't be bothered with that silly rule. See you in June, Jules." And he kissed me on the cheek, sauntering down the stairs, and out to the car parked in the circular driveway. I watched him climb into the front seat of his Mercedes, put the top down, shift it into gear and peel out. He screeched around the first corner and floored the engine.

At the same time that he paid my tuition to the school, he also defied the rules with his body. This was a subconscious lesson I learned. It would serve me well at sit-ins, at demonstrations, at teach-ins a few years later.

Students watch us with great scrutiny. They notice how we treat our colleagues, other students, the women who work in the office or who clean the floors. They are not always aware of what they take in at the time, just as I was not aware at the time of the permission my father seemed to be giving me.

It is summer. My father is driving me somewhere in a car. I am seventeen. He asks me what I know about sex. I say I know what is supposed to happen during sex, not telling him that I have come close to having first-hand experience, planned to have it soon, in love with my boyfriend, Tom, and how Tom moved over me, his tweed jacket on the floor of his surgeon father's library.

"Good. Glad you know," my father says. The moon seems to grin at us from the rearview mirror.

We ride in silence until he speaks suddenly, ten minutes later, saying that men can be unkind sometimes. It is up to the woman to stop this unkindness.

I absorb his message, feel slightly uneasy.

Speaking out loud about sex that night in the car as we went along was not easy for my father. He tried. What I took from his words was that there were many things I must never tell him. I would be blamed for whatever happened to me in the world of sexuality. Four years later, his instructions that night in the car provided the basis for a deep separation between us.

I wonder what messages I am sending my students, with the best of intentions. I remember being videotaped early in my career. Later, watching it with my advisor, she pointed out to me that when I turned away from one student, Mary, without responding to her question, in order to help another, Josh, Mary looked crestfallen. She did not work the rest of the hour. I had not seen that, and had not had the experience yet to sense it, to respond.

When I suggest to students that they lower their voice, or use different songs or words or language over and over again, am I implying something about what they hold dear? And yet how much of this is necessary and the right "way to behave" in a world that is primarily still run based on the way one group of people in power believe we should all behave? I also know students will be judged on this standard of behavior. How do I prepare them without stifling their enthusiasm, their love of motion, action, question, storytelling? This is our conundrum: this, our constant puzzle. And I let it rest here, in its ambivalent no-answer.

If I were Jewish and went to St Margaret's I would have stayed in the one single room, the way Susan Cohen did, and later the way a single black student stayed. This separation sent a message to us all.

Thus, I lived in a white ghetto both physically and mentally. I am not sure what we can ask of ourselves except to acknowledge a monochrome existence, if this is the way we have lived, admit to the "elusive things" of which DuBois speaks, and go back and probe in these crystalline days of true isolation.

And all that time, my father, while loving what this boarding school stood for, was urging me to question it. All that time he was not totally "sold" on this for his oldest child. By the fourth child, Claudia, he would insist she and his fifth and youngest stay home and go to public school. I believe he saw that we rebelled against the rigidity of our schools once we got to college and that perhaps a public school, everyday education, under his supervision and interaction, would keep these last two of his five children happier and less troublesome.

Decades after my high school graduation I brought a bouquet of flowers to class desk each Monday. I remembered the rooms of boarding school with their lilacs and roses and plants on tables, in windows. And each afternoon my students—Mai Xiong, Tameka Jones, Chris Olson, and Pa Vang—asked for one blossom when the day was over, a gift to bring to their homes. Flowers are one thing I kept from my days at St. Margaret's.

Recently I watched children and parents, community members and teachers gather in the library of an elementary school near where I live now in Minneapolis. There was an ease of entry, a coming and going that felt more natural than many of the buildings where I have taught or visited. Subconscious and almost imperceptible things—the way the front desk people spoke, the way the hall guards talked to the children, the skin color of the staff to a certain degree, added to fluidity between front door and neighborhood, between community and media center. My schooling, even at St. Margaret's, always felt like an extension of my life, a logical progression from home to institution. A version of this feeling is what the best schools seem conscious of and address in subtle and nuanced ways from food in the cafeteria to multilingual signs in the hallways.

Even then, where there was an all-white student body, I continued to glide by the *class* differences in front of me: the day students who had to eat in the locker room in the basement while boarders ate under chandeliers even for lunch, soup and sandwiches on silver platters at noontime. While I may have sensed that the day students did not have as much money as my family, I envied them for their ordinary days; I wanted to go home after school to a customary kitchen, fights about homework, and my mother's mediocre cooking.

Reflection: What messages did you learn about race subconsciously as you got older and could read and argue and talk with your parents?

Suggestion: Ask someone to tape a class you are having difficulty with. Watch it with a friend, mentor, coach. Look for subconscious messages you are sending to students through tone of voice, body language.

LESSON 21: INTIMATE EDUCATION

Confessions are difficult because they force me to visit ghettos in the mind I thought I had long escaped.

—*Kevin Powell, Who's Gonna Take the Weight?*

I want so much to skip over this part of my life. I would rather not reveal my response, my insensitivity. Yet here it is.

This story revolves around a Jewish girl named Judy. She came to live with the same family in Sweden that I was living with the summer after boarding school. We were part of a program called Experiment in International Living. She had a curved back that bent her in an unusual shape. She had black hair that bunched out from her head in wild array, dark eyes, and olive skin. Her nose was large, her mouth sweet smiling. We were staying with the Bondesons, a well-off family who spent summers on an island off Stockholm. I was paired up with Ulla, who was my age, eighteen. Judy was paired up with Eva, who was sixteen. I was from Connecticut, Judy from Texas.

I looked like the Bondesons. I was tall and blonde and blue-eyed with hair that fell (I thought glamorously) over one eye. This style not only drove my mother crazy, but Mrs. Bondeson as well. I came from beaches, they came from sailing and jumping off rocks into the cold Atlantic. Judy stood out, as an odd and distorted kid, yet in a body that was almost elderly. Eva made faces behind her back. Ulla laughed about her with me before we went to sleep. I remember seeing her comprehension and hurt when she caught on.

I also remember my discomfort with the whole scene. Remember feeling sorry for her, for her odd looks and odd religion, for her descriptions of Texas where I had spent two years of my life, a place my parents hated. I remember how kind Haaken was to her. He was a boy who lived on a nearby island and was in love with Eva. I remember how Judy did join in and jump off rocks nude and how good those days were for her.

Eventually, over the two months something softened all around her and took her in. Yet it was a different taking in than the one accorded to me. I was enveloped in a similarity with them all. I was part of four o'clock tea, pouring when it was my turn.

This was one of the most intimate times I had ever spent with anyone who was not like me, who was not Protestant, not from the East Coast. In my world she was "other." I did not do well. I did not object to her treatment, to the snide comments and the collusion among us to exclude her in subtle ways: turns of the shoulder, sarcastic tone of voice, condescension, and obsequiousness. To challenge this would have meant going against the community that surrounded me. I remember that Judy's Jewishness was part of the equation.

There were two other Jewish kids in our American group, Lesley and Peter. We all toured together at the end of the summer, and I noticed in those final weeks how happy Judy became. The flinch, the hurt was gone from her then, as she lay on the bed in hotel rooms talking with Lesley and Peter.

I stayed with the three of them much of the remainder of the travel time until we arrived back in the United States. What drove me to be with them then after being part of the scene that isolated Judy in July? I am not sure. I do know that Peter and Lesley were fascinating to me in their sophistication and knowledge of the world. I eavesdropped on their conversations about the Holocaust: their parents were survivors of death camps in Poland. And it seemed, in some indefinable way, that their experience was at a level *above* mine in its intimacy with the world, with reality itself. They seemed to exude a kind of roughness I wanted to have, a street knowledge of New York, Chicago. I wanted to be with them simply to be exposed to it.

And when they included Judy, I included Judy. They asked her questions about Texas, about being Jewish there, about how she celebrated holidays. She became more and more eager and interesting, less and less dependent.

At this age I switched allegiances easily. My adolescence had been, in a certain sense, far delayed. I was just emerging into struggles many kids had been having throughout their high school lives. My real regret, though, from that time, is that I did not make more of an effort to break from the mocking, subtle rejection of Judy for the two months we lived on the island.

"Here is how you are if you are fair," Lesley and Peter said to me in how they behaved. I went along because I wanted to listen to discussions of politics, history, family. For the time being I wanted to *be* them.

In Sweden at first I had nothing to lose and everything to gain by teasing Judy. Because I was so much the same as those in the family with whom I lived I could easily slip into association with them. And I did. How often we see students who are wavering in this way: sometimes between being cool with their peers and yet at the same time wanting to get into a rigorous academic tract. For some kids, wanting to get a good education may find them being accused of giving up on their culture or friends. I have known students who arrange with teachers to turn in papers and complete work without letting their peers know that they are succeeding so that they won't be teased, won't be put down or even harassed for doing well. I am also convinced that this veneer, of toughness on the part of those who tease the ones doing well, is very thin. Students who ended up confiding with me over the years, and who were often in serious trouble for defiance and refusal to work, expressed a secret admiration for those who were attempting to "make it out" as they said.

I am reminded that our brains, our value systems are not formed completely until we are nineteen. I also know that young people, from thirteen to seventeen are trying not only to figure out their identities as students, as cultural beings, as religious people, but are also trying to determine right and wrong, good or bad. It is a time of impulsiveness too, a time they change from sensible to irrational in a single day, a long afternoon, one class hour.

As teachers we have a chance to help them form a way of figuring out their ethical lives. We can do it by modeling and we can do it by having students, similar to them in many ways, be part of their learning. Some schools combine grade levels for tutoring or mentoring. Some enlist high school junior and seniors to guide younger students, meet them after one class and walk them to the next one in order to keep them from skipping. I remember setting up a high school basketball hero, who was also excellent in academics, to meet one of my troubled ninth graders after second hour and walk him to third hour, a class he often missed. Because Brett was willing to be the escort, it worked.

If we could create a vibrant school culture that combined Spoken Word Poetry in with Yeats or Shakespeare, combined neighborhood work on environmental issues with the science of wind pattern for examples, perhaps we could create a school that was so hip, so cool, so relevant to the streets and communities that many more students would want to come. Combine that with peers encouraging other peers to get to class and we could turn around the dissatisfaction and disconnect so many urban students feel between their lives and education. There are many examples of where this is happening, where students and parents do not feel "other" as they enter the door to the building.

Because the other is only in relation to the observer, Judy was not other to Lesley and Peter and was not treated as such. Looking at this summer now I realize it was a time when I learned that I was raised to see beauty or truth or goodness in a certain limited way. I learned different ways of defining this from my peers. By using this influence of child to child, group to individual instead of continually fighting it, we might find ways to change attitudes toward race, culture, school itself. Models of antiracist behavior are there among students as well as adults.

Reflection: Think of a time when you did not act to stop teasing, racist jokes, words, or actions against certain people or a person. What did you learn from this? How has it influenced you?

Suggestions: Organize cross-age tutoring, class to class escort services, and student leadership teams that will influence seventh, eighth, or ninth graders at a crucial time in their development. Use peers to influence peers, trying to be sensitive to how this will seem, and develop ways to counter negativism. Brainstorm with supportive colleagues what a supportive, hip school might be like.

LESSON 22: EXPECTATIONS

After St. Margaret's I went on to a women's college, a logical extension for me at the time. My first year at Wheaton College, Massachusetts, nestled in the hills of some of the most stunning autumn leaves in the country, I found myself on familiar ground. We studied the culture and history of Europe. We studied French and classical music. We studied Shakespeare and Jane Austen. The time I was at Wheaton (1962 to 1964) was a time when people of color were perceived and portrayed by the media as part of the "issues" of the day. I had headed straight into Peggy McIntosh's "people of color as problems, as issue" category of education. The news of anger and protest and courage surrounded me.

That first fall four little girls were killed in the bombing of the Birmingham church in Alabama. Do I remember hearing about this, remember the moment when I looked up and saw it on television or the words over a radio? I do not. A year later I would learn of Kennedy's assassination and I can tell you that dark skies and rain of a November day descended with a great silence and sadness on the car in which I was riding to the Yale versus Harvard weekend. I can tell you where I was when Robert Kennedy was shot years after that, but not when Medgar Evers was killed on his front step.

I wonder if it still has to do with the luxury of *not knowing*. I did not know because what happened to those who were black did not happen to me, to "my people." I do believe when I heard of it I absorbed the news of Birmingham with sadness.

That I could continue not knowing, not being involved that year, had to do with the whiteness of this college. Many young women were there because their mothers went to Wheaton. In two years my sister would attend Connecticut College where my mother had gone. And in these stone buildings, in these arched bridges, we were welcomed "legacies," as the daughters of those who came before, as those who looked like the daughters of those who came before. Legacies continue today in colleges, prep schools, law schools, and med schools. Yet rarely are they described as a kind of affirmative action.

Some students at Carleton College in Northfield, Minnesota, have told me that their grades and test scores were not anywhere near as good as many of their classmates. Because their parents attended Carleton, they were admitted, while other colleges had turned them down. Because people of color were denied entry into these colleges and universities for years they are not often part of the "network" of legacy that can get you in.

If our students come into our high school or even middle school class inexplicably angry some day, while it may be because they didn't get enough sleep or they had a fight with their father, it may also be one of those days when they sense something like this legacy system, they sense that the deck is stacked.

Despite the environment at Wheaton, something new began there for me that first year. I met Cheryl Simms. Cheryl was light skinned and black identified. Denise Jefferson went to this college too, and she was dark skinned and politically involved in the fight to integrate Boston schools. In watching them and in talking with them I began to see differences between us and to know where I could engage in dialogue.

My parents jokingly said that after five children they figured that it was about the third day of the second month of our sophomore year that the kids of Boone and Susie Guyton began to challenge them and in some cases began the separation from their way of life. As much as they joked about it, we *did* all seem to wake up in college. We turned toward the streets or worked down south or traveled to Africa or Eastern Europe.

During my first year I broke from my family in my social behavior. I began to get to know Cheryl and Denise. I began to seriously date a white young man named Tom Cole, who went to an unknown small college in Springfield, Massachusetts. In getting to know Tom I developed a secret life. In preparation for other secrets that I would guard almost all my years, I learned to live on night streets, walk city blocks, take midnight trains.

This was 1963 when even in the civil rights movement women were given secondary status. At this time they were fighting assumptions about their role as secretary, dishwasher, or girlfriend and demanding to be a part of the decision making, the activism, the teaching and registering voters in this movement.

When students come into our classes who are fighting their own battles around gender issues as many young women are, this resonates. In some ways white women have a chance to understand discrimination or lowered expectations that white men do not have because of our experiences of limitations or even harassment due to our gender.

Shane Price, head of the African American Men project, tells me that allies throughout his life have often been white women. This does not guarantee an understanding of racism. Yet there is a history of powerful women, both white and black, and the alliances they have made in contexts from antislavery and abolitionist work to community development to voting rights. This is a history many students never read about, never hear about when they study the civil rights movement.

By February of my second year at Wheaton I went into Boston to help run Freedom Schools. These were part of the boycott of city schools by blacks who had been asking for equal access to good education, either in their own neighborhoods or in busing to good schools. Louise Day Hicks, notorious school superintendent, fought any effort at integration of the city schools.

Denise Jefferson organized those of us who volunteered to help out in various locations where alternative classrooms had been created during the boycott. I remember riding the train with Denise, watching her from afar and being fascinated. She was fired up, laughing, singing as we rode. Other black and white students surrounded her, some quietly smiling at her exuberance, some reading, some singing along. Denise had her hair in a natural Afro, shaped around her head in a cloud of black curl. At the time this seemed exotic. We taught some students for a few days and left when the boycott was over. It felt natural to me to do this work. I had done some tutoring when I went to St. Margaret's and schools—even those created hastily in storefronts—were comfortable places for me.

Those I respect in the education field like to talk about *action learning* versus *service learning*. They stress that if we have students out in their own communities, organizing violence prevention classes, working for adequate housing, trying to get a drug clinic built, or a garden and park put in, we can engage them as early as fourth grade. If we had them acting instead of sitting, the shear physical movement might rouse some of them to hope.

I have heard students talk about what they learned, what they saw, and what influence it had on them when they worked for fair housing in tenth grade, or for voter registration in high school. I taught a group of seventh graders who were so moved by the plight of child laborers in Nepal after a doctor/photographer came to talk with our class, they decided to have a benefit rock concert for a school in that country that was being built to accommodate elementary-aged bricklayers.

By the end of my second spring at Wheaton I had decided to transfer to George Washington University because I wanted to be where the marches and demonstrations were happening, to be where the action was. Denise had something to do with that, I know.

The summer between Wheaton and George Washington, Vince Ceglie (an Italian man from Dorchester, an Italian and African American section of Boston, who was thirty years old) and I were walking up to my parents' house by the ocean. We had spent hours that night jumping through phosphorescent fish in the midnight water of the surf. As we came around a curve in the path from the beach and turned to climb the final hill, I looked up in the window. My father stared down at us. Because of the light that shone behind him I could only sense his frown. When I walked into the kitchen he stood directly across from us. No one said anything. Eventually, he turned and walked toward the bedroom where my mother was sleeping. He did not approve of my new man, a "wop" he called Vince later.

His silence that night, that abrupt turn on his heel, signaled his defeat.

I wonder now what I would have been like if I did not have Dad to rebel against. Poor man, he drove me exactly where he did not want me to go. It is ironic that without my father's silent disapproval, without his anger and his "kike" or "wop" or "nigger," I might not have found the man who ultimately became my husband, might not have found the work that sustains me, even in the most troubled times. It feels odd to be grateful to my father for his prejudice, for his anger.

Just before I left for Washington, DC, in the summer of 1964, the bodies of three civil rights workers, Michael Schwerner, James Chaney, and Andrew Goodman, were found stuffed in the banks of the river in Philadelphia, Mississippi. They had been shot in cold blood while working to register voters. Their parents stunned me in their outspoken anger, grief, courage, and in their support of what their own sons were trying to do. This story accompanied me to "super dorm" at George Washington.

It was truly the activism, the action of learning on the streets of Boston that drove me to change schools and altered my life radically. It lit a fire under me. I can't help but feel something like this is needed now to light that fire under our high school students of all ethnicities.

Reflection: Think of a time when you were an activist working for change. What motivated you? Where did it lead? Was it part of your church work? Neighborhood or community work?

Suggestions: Conduct a survey of needs, issues, or concerns among your students and their parents. Brainstorm projects with them after you look at the results of the surveys. What might you focus on? Help students become realistic. Combine this with research, writing, and artistic subjects for credit.

5

Alliances, Risks, and Starting Over

LESSON 23: CONNECTING TO REALITY

It is warm, a DC fall that shines like no other, with blue skies and southern nights. I begin my junior year at George Washington University (GWU). To my parents' credit they paid my way here, even though they did not understand my reasons for leaving a good woman's college in a protected hamlet of Massachusetts, for a second-rate university in the middle of a city my father hated after all his work in aviation at the Pentagon.

I am standing outside a civil rights office, home of tutoring, political activity, and the United Campus Christian Ministries office, all rolled into one. I am leaning on a car, waiting as the sky darkens, for the office to open. A young white man, Bill, stands next to me and we talk, about politics, about arriving in DC from different colleges. When the crew cut white minister opens the door, Bill and I go in and chat with him for a while, and sign up to tutor. My companion, Bill Fletcher, walks me toward my dorm, after a beer or two at Brownlies on Pennsylvania Avenue. We kiss in an alleyway between two row houses before I go to my dorm for the night.

Looking back on that slowly descending night, on the circles of the city I grew to love, on the young woman there, walking these streets too casually, I can't help but marvel at my luck. I had been feeling, up until then, an inarticulate restlessness. And it was that vague emotion that had propelled me even on my first night into this more activist place.

Over the course of the fall, I spent hours in that storefront office, running next door for sandwiches at the deli, smoking cigarettes into the morning, talking politics, planning marches, meeting white men and women, some of whom had already been in Mississippi registering voters.

George Washington was a white southern university. Many of those who lead and attended this institution considered segregation as the way of the world. The year I arrived, this assumption was challenged. The week I began classes, a group of senior white women, some of them officers, walked out of their sororities because alumnae had overruled their selection of Jewish girls to these same sororities. In an odd juxtaposition I participated in Rush Week, intending to join a sorority on Monday, and walked the protest line outside the sorority houses by Friday.

Soon after these initial weeks I went to a little town in Virginia called Gum Springs where we worked with Reverend Haskins on voter registration and fair housing causes. Here I saw shacks with dirt floors where children and parents slept in one bed, a wood burning stove that barely kept out the bone chilling cold of Northern Virginia winters. Often, there were fires in these structures and they went up in flames in a matter of minutes. A number of us worked on fair housing for people in this part of Virginia, located on George Washington's former plantation. We worked with the reverend to solicit signatures for various petitions, to transport people to meetings of county commissioners, housing department bureaucrats. Other issues of concern to those in the community were medical services and birth control for the women who lived in Gum Springs.

In this work I learned more than any textbook would tell me about history and poverty. I surveyed those in Gum Springs about the conditions they lived in, helped get medical information to them, assisted Bill Hobbs, a fellow activist, in publishing the Gum Springs newspaper. I began my work against the Viet Nam war, reading background and history to be prepared for interviews or actions with peace groups. I encountered men both white and black who were helpful and men who wanted to hit on women in the civil rights movement. I began to sort out the complexity involved in being a white woman even in equity and social justice work.

All of this was *physical*. It was being in the communities involved. It was organizing and being present at teach-ins about the war. It was negotiating with African Americans who were angry with us privileged whites who were getting more commendation than they had ever received for the hard work they had been doing around these issues long before we came along. It was a time of discomfort or hurt as a result of tough discussions and confrontations.

Similar work with middle and high school students is equally important for their intellectual and emotional growth. Schools whose staff and teachers view themselves as directors of a place for their students to research situations, write up experiences, and back up these experiences with facts and anecdote are hard to resist. By continuing the dialogue that arises from this research and contact with the community center or church, synagogue or mosque, teachers give meaning to students' education, truly crossing the boundaries between home and school. This is not only action learning, but is a step toward activist learning.

There are teachers who take classes out to test the water in their city lakes, or to work in a homeless shelter or to study the nutrition in foods provided by federal programs for the poor. There are amazing principals who speak at churches, in library dialogues or at city council meetings about what is needed in their schools, and in the neighborhoods. In these buildings students become energized, not only to complete the project, but to learn the intricacies involved, be it the science of the body, the life of bacteria in water, or the funding of grants in nutrition and education.

This work can be the basis for demanding academic work. It can be a way of raising expectations. It can also drive a real change in institutional racism. Advanced Placement classes could be redefined to include literature, projects, and research that coalesces around concerns in the community where a school resides.

Reflection: When was a time you took your students outside the classroom? When was a time you challenged tracking in your school?

Suggestion: Organize a continuing dialogue with colleagues and students about institutional racism, perpetuation of privilege, and how to break this pattern. Assume it will be uncomfortable and will take time.

LESSON 24: MAKING MISTAKES

When I went home from George Washington I rarely mentioned what I was doing. If I ever brought up civil rights or anti–Viet Nam war activity my father came down on me with such fury I eventually kept silent.

"Why do you want to go rile things up? Those people going down South and doing that stuff are just asking for trouble."

"Vote? Eventually they will vote, but they aren't ready for that yet!"

I could not even begin to argue with this man.

At George Washington I was dropped into the literal center of debate about black and white, war and peace.

Meanwhile one of my roommates would say she did not like the color pink because it was a "Negro color."

Meanwhile I danced with black men one day in Gum Springs when we stopped for lunch at a small store and music came on the plastic radio on the shelf above the freezer. I did this because I thought it was "cool" and radical to dance with black men. Later, the leaders of the civil rights group would reprimand me for this attitude and inform me about the danger still of black men–white women combinations. I was risking the lives of all who were there that day. After all, Emmet Till had been killed for barely glancing at a white woman only nine years earlier.

The reprimand stung. I was continually being asked to rethink assumptions, rethink what others had, did not have, where they were allowed to safely go, to be effective in my work.

I learned with my body, and with my emotions in response to criticism. We have missed out, and more important, our students have missed out, on many ways of learning, on Howard Gardner's many kinds of intelligences and their nurturing. This lesson I learned with my emotions, with my reactions, and it taught me whole new concepts and social skills.

Those in the George Washington group with me were white, twenty, and in love with each other and the work, yet oblivious in some ways to our white privilege even then. As people died and bodies were found in river banks, as Malcolm X was shot and marchers were beaten with batons and bitten by dogs, we were swept up into primarily white versions of all this. We did interact with black men and women at parties where workers arrived in DC for a break from the South, exhausted by the constant danger they had been living under in Mississippi and Alabama, Georgia and Louisiana.

It was a heady time when reporters came to ask us questions at meetings of the Liberal Education Action Project (LE/AP) or Students for a Democratic Society (SDS), or the antiwar moratorium assemblies. Many of these newsmen were fresh from down South too and some even bullet torn.

We thrived on hope. We believed that our work for peace and racial justice would succeed, that we would "win." We went into social action with the faith others have in their churches: that righteousness would triumph and be rewarded. We had the unshakable belief that if we just talked to people enough, just pointed out the injustices in voting, housing, education, heath care, we would triumph. And who can fault this belief? Not me. I am not writing to decry that young woman who worked hours and hours in that office with the torn leather couch or out in Gum Springs tutoring or walking dirt roads.

Yet I want it to be clear here that my wild faith, my willingness to go places with a kind of fearlessness that was foolish, came partly from my privileged upbringing, my lack of acquaintance with defeat. How fortunate then that I was welcomed by Chris Hobbs, Dick Yeo, Ed Bauers, Ed Knappman, Maury Landsman in the LE/AP office. How lucky for me that my dorm fees were all paid for, my tuition covered.

Contrary to my college situation, for urban students tuition funding has often not been available. Advise about getting on a college track has not been possible in schools where a counselor's caseload can be as high as five hundred students. Some counselors do not believe black students or poor students can make it in college anyway, and in their own subtle ways discourage students. Others want to make more information available but end up spending all their time scheduling students into already overcrowded classrooms. And often in schools with few resources, computers and software are not available for students to explore on their own. It seems to me we need a resurgence, a civil rights type education movement in the United States.

Civil rights workers in Mississippi and Alabama went to the small churches, the front porches of those they were organizing to vote. Teachers and school workers might go to the plant where many of the kids' parents work. In some imaginative districts superintendents open up buildings and have school into the evenings, not only to provide extra time on the few computers they do have, but to offer working adults in the community who do not have their high school diplomas a chance to take classes toward getting one. Teachers in some schools, by demanding that students who do not have the usual excellent grade point averages be admitted to their Advanced Placement (AP) classes anyway, are changing the racial and ethnic composition of these classes in their individual schools.

Do we need help with this? Do we need money and resources, small class sizes and social workers, activists and decent working conditions for teachers? There is no doubt we do. We need help from community members and parents too. We need to have our assumptions, our judgments challenged. I was lucky to have this happen early in my life.

"What formed you?" adults often ask, as I give talks or read from my work on education. I am trying to tell it here. I am trying to trace this welcoming world: how I intersected, did not intersect with the poor or brown or black communities all around me. I marched and I picketed and I traveled. I made stupid mistakes and was told about them.

I wonder now if the chaos of it, the whirlwind of it, was not the best thing that could have happened. For a moment in history alliances were formed around a common cause. We accepted each other despite our grave mistakes. Today some of our schools feel like similar whirlwinds. Young teachers and new teachers continue to amaze me with their energy, their resilience. We don't want to lose them. We don't want to lose the first grade teacher who brings food each day for students who miss breakfast or the science teacher who scrounges up money to get water-testing equipment for his students to go down to the Mississippi River and draw samples. We don't want to lose the math and English teachers who work together in an interdisciplinary exercise to teach "The Pit and the Pendulum" by Edgar Allen Poe and then take their students outside to measure the rate at which the pendulum might drop by asking a city worker to bring a derrick to the football field for that purpose. In all the difficulty of generating amazing lessons, these teachers flourish. They make mistakes and they come right back. They come possessing a certain brazen hope.

Reflection: What gives you hope in your school? Do you have a different relationship with this emotion than your students or their families do? Articulate what that is, what might have made this difference.

Suggestions: How can you literally and physically extend school into the community. Could parents take classes at your high school for their GED? Could you set up an evening tutoring service for parents who are English Language Learners (ELL)?

LESSON 25: UNTOLD STORIES, UNHEARD VOICES

Just the week before I would join the end of the march from Selma to Montgomery with Martin Luther King, Maury Landsman, who would eventually become my husband, and I were sitting amidst a group of protestors at the Department of Justice on Pennsylvania Avenue. Along with the whole country, the attorney general of the United States had seen the pictures of the dogs tearing at the bones of men and women and children on the Pettis Bridge outside Selma. We blocked his office with hundreds of others demanding he send troops to protect King and the marchers. We linked arms and sang songs.

"Ain't gonna let nobody turn me 'roun', turn me 'roun', turn me 'roun'."

Ray Robinson was sitting on my right. After walking from Canada to Cuba on a civil rights march, after being beaten and jailed time after time because of his extraordinary size, his rich voice, and his dark black color, he went crazy when the uniforms descended. He warned me that when the cops came, I must let go of his arm, that if I kept hold of his arm, he might toss me around. If his arms flailed up and out into the air, and I kept staying next to him, he might hurt me without meaning to.

"We shall not, we shall not be moved, we shall not, we shall not be moved."

Maury was one row ahead of me. He went out just before I did, carried by one cop on each side. Later, he would tell me he leaned on the elevator to keep it open so they could not bring everyone down. Finally the cops figured out what was happening. They pushed him to the side and closed the door. When they got to the first floor, more cops took protesters out, dragging them down the steps by their feet, their heads bouncing on the granite, as mine would do a few moments later.

"Just like a tree that's standing by the water, we shall not be moved."

When the cops came, I did just as Ray told me. I let go. His body jerked up and down. It took six men to subdue him. Just before they came for me, I watched Ray become inert, dragged out of the room.

As one cop came, toward me on my right and another on my left, I looked directly into their faces. The one on the right was black, and as I smiled at him, I could see tears start to run down his cheeks. He lifted me with more gentleness than the cop on my left who was white. All the while they dragged me down the hall and into the elevator, the black man wept. Weeks earlier I had seen the same tears on the face of another black cop as we tried to go by him to get closer to the White House.

Later that evening after the Justice Department sit-in, I found my way home to Maury's apartment. I remember a March drizzle, with a hint of flowers. As I saw the light on in his room, up above me, I felt something new, something settling.

A few days later I went to Montgomery, Alabama, on a train with hundreds of others. Maury had decided not to go on this trip, having become already disillusioned with large demonstrations. Many of those who had worked in the civil rights movement were not sure such large gatherings were working. While they brought media attention to the lack of freedom, they also aroused danger and hatred. I was not convinced it was time to stop such massive marches. Maury, a more seasoned veteran of confrontations in Delaware and Maryland, was working in nearby communities and on university policy. I understood by then that one way of being active did not exclude the other.

After the end of King's march into Montgomery from Selma was over, I climbed onto the train around four in the afternoon, exhausted from the heat of the city and no sleep for two days. Out of the train windows we could see FBI agents patroling alongside the cars, their walkie-talkies squawking in the dust and heat. When we finally arrived home in the DC railroad station we were told of the death of a white housewife from Detroit, Viola Liuzzo, and a black man, Leroy Moton, who were driving home the night after the march.

All thoughts of jubilation vanished. The reality of so many of the white and black men and women, children and elders, and the danger they still faced struck us immediately. Combined with those furious men and women we had seen lined up along Montgomery's suburban and urban streets just hours before, thoughts of celebration or congratulation disappeared.

Students still want to hear stories from these times. I am always surprised by their reaction when I mention this experience of the march. Even the more jaded young women and men in alternative schools want to hear more.

"Did you shake hands with King?"

"Did anybody spit on you, call you names?"

"Was it hot?"

"What were trains like then?"

The younger ones want to shake the hand that shook the hand of King, others want to know what music was like back then and what did people shout from the side of the street.

Any description of this action, this activism must be accompanied by recognition of all those who gave up their lives years and years *before* Selma, before King, before the march, for this struggle. The line of deaths from slave ships to plantations, to civil war to reconstruction to voter rights shootings have created a history of courage that is rarely taught to our children, white and black. And the lack of white heroes and heroines, like Viola Liuzzo and Casey Hayden who worked at a very young age in Mississippi towns that were hidden and thus especially dangerous, is a serious problem. The lack of depth in teaching about the civil rights struggles and the alliances between white and blacks, newspaper editors and judges, ministers and professors is a glaring gap in the education of all students.

If we do read about that march to Montgomery I participated in, we do not hear about what happened to the men and women from Montgomery who joined the march and lost their jobs the next day. How tilted even the textbook history of the civil rights movement is, toward certain years, certain white heroes, white stories. What happened to those blacks who gave up rooms in their homes, food at their table, the basements of churches, to civil rights workers? Were there whites who did this?

It seems that embedded in a complete narrative of this time is the important story of alliances, a time when we worked together, marched together in larger numbers. What better lesson to show our kids than this, that we can locate ourselves in places of action together. What a loss to them, all of them, white and black, when this story is neglected. What a fine time to bring both white and black heroes of real relevance to students in every kind of school.

The finest teachers ignore the textbook that does not present this story. Rather they create their own material, create their own simulations, topics, projects. This is tricky in a time of prescribed and proscribed curriculum, mandated books, constant oversight. Yet those teachers who read James Loewen's wonderful books on history, who consult Howard Zinn and *Rethinking Schools* publications are in every city, every system. They need support for this work, for their imagination, their tireless search for truth and provocative and demanding ways of presenting these truths. They are the same teachers who are fearless in encouraging tough discussions of race in the classroom.

Joel Dressler, a white man who joined our civil rights group around this time after working in Kentucky with miners and in Alabama with voter registration workers, showed me what it meant to take activism to another level and to see what was really happening around me.

Joel became enraged when Brownlies Bar, our hangout that year, refused to serve a black man a beer. Joel was kicked out along with the man.

I had loved that bar, with its wooden booths and its frosty pitchers that came up golden and cold to our table. I loved the French fries and the jukebox at each booth and the way we could fit six of us in together, another group in the booth across. I loved the light of Pennsylvania Avenue as we emerged each evening.

Yet after Joel was literally thrown out on his back for challenging the refusal to serve blacks in that place, we knew we could never go back. It had taken Joel to make us aware of what was missing from this neighborhood place: no black faces after work, no one nursing a glass of beer at the bar after a hard day. And perhaps it was Joel, with his awareness of such absences, his way of seeing what was *not* there, that taught me as much as all the marches and speeches and organizing put together. He taught me that it is action with your body and your voice *in the everyday* that matters the most.

Many teachers and educational assistants of color have said to me that what especially frustrates them is that after private agreement with white colleagues about what is needed in a building or school program, when it comes to saying this out loud in a faculty meeting or before a school board, these same colleagues are not there, do not "have their back." This is especially egregious because it is still the case that when a white teacher brings up a solution to a problem in our schools, he or she will often have more credibility with his or her colleagues, even if the issue is about black studies or Latino literature.

Yet it is our privileged status to sit back. We can weigh whether we want to risk losing friends, giving up our favorite bar, offending someone in power. White kids already see teachers who look like them and books that include them and examples that applaud the accomplishments of those with their skin color. Yet we also know that white kids who are not taught Latino history or Asian literature, who do not have a balanced view of accomplishment and cultural celebration lose out, too. Even given this, we disappear when the time comes to advocate for a different textbook, or fail to speak up about the over-referral of black boys to special education classes.

Until there is a history of action, of putting ourselves out there despite the hostility of some of our fellow teachers, we will not have earned the trust of colleagues of color, or even white activists. And not only colleagues but students notice who stands with them, who is willing to challenge them, tell them the truth, put up with some loss of affection from powers that be if necessary.

Joel taught me this. Yet I have not always followed what I learned from him. It resonates now, when I think on those days when it seemed that each day I learned from failure or from revelation.

Reflection: What did you learn about the civil rights movement when you were in school? Growing up? What did you learn about all that went on before: the partition of Africa, slavery, Reconstruction, abolitionism? When was a time you challenged prescribed curriculum? When you supported colleagues' demands for change? When you didn't?

Suggestion: Create a text that is an alternative to your assigned book. Use the regular text as a way for students to explore what is *not* included.

LESSON 26: ERRORS AND CORRECTIONS

The summer after this tumultuous first year at GWU, I moved into Maury's apartment. I worked for a DC redevelopment agency. My job was to walk the streets of Northeast Washington and take a census of those who lived in this area. This was a part of the city that was scheduled to be torn down to make room for condos and high-end housing. In my gratitude in finding a job I did not learn much about its purpose. I knocked on doors and found women still in bed after the night shift at a nearby hospital; I went into attics where men played chess while rats wandered the floors at their feet. I saw some of the worst conditions I had ever seen, right near the capitol dome, gleaming on the horizon. My job was also to find out if any of these places needed repairs and to report those needs. This was a preliminary survey and people would be paying rent in these buildings for years before the actual wrecking ball arrived.

Here, African Americans surrounded me and here, even in an area described by the media as crime ridden, I felt safe. Was this naiveté, this ease I felt walking streets in DC, changing buses to get across the city to work, stopping on the way at a black restaurant for doughnuts and coffee? I don't think so. I think it was realistic. There were working people and stoop-sitting people and tired and frustrated and shop-owner people where I worked. Not one of them got angry toward me for the news I brought about their eventual eviction.

During this summer I also worked on a bus boycott in DC. The transit system in the city was leaving whole sections of the black community off its routes.

I spent a Sunday with Marion Berry, later a controversial mayor and legislator, then a civil rights worker who was helping organize a strike of bus riders. We hid behind corners of buildings as big silver buses pulled to stops, and then ran out with our strike bumper stickers and put them on the bus just as it was lurching out onto the street.

After a few early morning hours of this Marion took me to little church after little church in the basements of houses or in storefronts. One was the Jesus Only church, the members not believing in God, but rather devoting their belief and work to Jesus alone. While I had been in similar churches on my job, this time I was going into the places at their time of singing and worship and asking for support for the boycott. At first Marion did the talking, his voice a powerful one in the small rooms. After we had been to three churches, he turned the talk over to me, with a slight smile at my startled response to his introduction. I wavered in the beginning, yet soon my voice became louder than it has ever been, calling out and getting a chorus of "Amen, Sister" in response. By the end of the day I was into the swing of it.

When we got back to the headquarters Marion was laughing out loud. He told the group that I had gotten them singin' and a yessin' with me, and I sounded like a "real sister." I laughed with the group at the office and went back to my apartment, a slight bit more confident in my ability to negotiate unknown territory.

Was I aware of my whiteness yet? Yes. Not in an analytical or an intellectual way. But, oh yes, I was aware that I was the only white person in certain rooms at certain times. I was aware that I was a white woman on black streets, checking out homes and kitchens and even the bullet wound of a man who staggered up to me one late afternoon when I happened to be out working one section with my black friend and coworker Ed McCampbell.

It was during this time, 1965, I learned not to use the word "colored." Ed and Cheryl Simms, the Wheaton student who had transferred to George Washington with me, preferred "Negro" and finally told me so. In being corrected, while it burnt, my cheeks flushing up to think of all the times I had said "colored" that same summer, being corrected was a constant part of my existence then.

And the reason this worked, the reason such correction "took" was that all during this time of training for tear gas, of curling into a ball to protect myself if the cops came, of parties where I joined hands and sang with Ray Robinson, all the things I was told, debated, talked about, I experienced in a community.

I think that the intimate work days of my life, the constant going out in the evening to meetings in all parts of the city, interchanges with a black boss and black coworkers, is what created the confidence in me to do the work I have done the rest of my life. I still make plenty of mistakes, still make erroneous assumptions based on skin color or religious garb or appearance. What this summer did, however, was convince me that I could live and work in any place with any group of people and enjoy it.

This augurs for residency requirements for teachers. Perhaps it does not have to be a requirement, but it can be encouraged as a way in to the kind of connection that teachers can make to be effective in urban schools. Some of my favorite teachers, black and white, are those who have become committed to the city where they teach.

My father would not pay anything for my living in DC that summer as he had wanted me to come home between junior and senior years. So for the first time I was earning my own living. Yet I had a reserve. In the back of my mind I knew this. I always had a fallback all my life because I knew my parents would not let me starve. I was still *white* white, with the financial cushion to go with it.

All around me in DC were people working their way through school, taking on extra jobs to make ends meet, planning on saving for books over their summers. I believe I was insensitive to the persistence of poverty, to the continual edginess and uncertainty it brought into the lives of those who lived with it. Yet I know too that there was an invisible knapsack of economic gifts, of economic privilege that accompanied me.

Reflection: In what ways have you been exposed to poverty? In working with students who live in poverty? How has either wealth or financial stability affected your life? How has poverty influenced you? Read the novel *Highwire Moon* by Susan Straight or the nonfiction book *Random Family* by Adrian Nicole LeBlanc, to go deeper into the experience.

Suggestion: Look over the sidebar that outlines suggestions for working with students in poverty. How is your building doing in this regard?

STRATEGIES FOR MEETING THE NEEDS OF ECONOMICALLY STRUGGLING STUDENTS

Assume all students can learn and can learn complicated and creative material.

Build a classroom and a school that gives control to students as much as possible while at the same time maintaining safety and structure. Allow their voices and interests to drive your curriculum.

Check on your own assumptions about poor kids or their parents: do not assume they are not as smart as other kids, that they do not want to learn, that they cannot learn in creative and unusual ways. Do not assume they all learn in one way or must be taught in a rote method at the expense of teaching them ways of thinking critically, writing creatively, or learning the scientific method, the Pythagorean theorem.

Think of the assets students who live in poverty bring to the classroom, not always the deficits. Resiliency, perseverance, flexibility, compassion, and even hope are just a few of the things some of these kids and their parents have learned.

Do not believe in stereotypes of poor students, or generalize about them. Use information and data to understand situations yet be careful of assuming behaviors or states of mind for any whole group. This becomes dangerously close to stereotyping.

Become reflective and self-reflective about why kids are without so much in our cities and neighborhoods. Don't be afraid to question the assumptions of others about these kids and their families. Be willing to speak up when destructive or negative comments are made about any whole group. Avoid the poison of the teachers' lounge if that is the way it is in your school.

Ask yourself: What do I control? Who are my allies? And go from there. Understand you cannot change the world, but can work within your classroom and community to create change. Be willing to really look at what you control: the building itself, the curriculum, the presence or absence of music as part of your curriculum.

Support teachers and colleagues who are challenging students and who are finding ways to reach them. Build a support network for those teachers in your building. Find ways for them to connect even if it is once a week by e-mail, or in the media center talking about "what went right this week" each Friday. Be imaginative about this support.

Remember, deciding on what to do in schools does not mean making the decision between treating kids like human beings versus academic and skill achievement.

Keep your own boundaries clear when working with students in trouble or who are in need of so much. Maintain your "other life" so that you can go into the classroom wholeheartedly, ready to meet kids with your heart and mind and without resentment. This is what they need from you the most.

Expand the notion of school functions: Can schools provide evening support groups for parents? Can they develop evening classes for both students who need credits and parents who also want to learn or get high school credit? Can they provide childcare for parents who want to come to conferences, transport parents to meetings, or even hold conferences in another location? Can teachers visit the neighborhoods from which their students come? The list here is endless.

Find ways to provide the basic necessities: a place to wash clothes; a winter coat drive for students; breakfast, snack, and lunch programs; funding from businesses for supplies, computers, keyboards, art materials.

Do not assume all kids have computers, phones, a regular place to live, access to pencils, books, supplies, enough food, a place to wash clothes, a feeling of safety when they go home, a place to fall asleep when they are tired.

Look in the community for the resources for kids: small churches that can provide a place to do homework, a community leader the kids respect, a shop where kids' parents go to talk and hang out.

Find a way to survey students at the beginning of the year or your class time with them. In this way you will learn a lot about their home situation.

Ask students to do jobs for you, making them feel important and also in control of something in their lives.

Do not single kids out or even indicate in front of others that you know they are homeless or poor, yet make yourself available for them to come in and talk with you. Refer them for help when this happens.

While you do not want to coddle students, you may also "cut deals" with some of them. If they do not bring their homework in some day because they had been out at night trying to find a place to sleep, figure out a time to help them get the homework done in school. Thus you are not letting them get away with not doing it at all, but you are making a deal with them about how to get it done.

Convince students, in whatever capacity you hold in a building: "I mean business. I believe you can learn and I will listen to you, giving you meaningful work to do." Provide them with a way to work at their level to achieve a grade, helping them increase skills without frustrating them. Make assignments open-ended.

Counsel other teachers who do not believe all students can learn.

LESSON 27: ALLIANCES

When I arrived in DC for my senior year in the fall of 1965, I moved into a house in Georgetown with five white women. We knew each other from various contexts at George Washington and found a house about twenty minutes' walk from campus. It was a house with old velvet furniture and long doors that opened off the dining room into the backyard below us. It became a gathering place.

It was a house where Stokely Carmichael, who later changed his name to Ture, came with Joel to a party early in the fall. I remember that Stokely

walked in, handsome and magnetic, one of the leading black civil rights workers from the Student Nonviolent Coordinating Committee (SNCC) who was
arguing for the change to an all-black organization. He watched us drinking
and talking. He took in the scene, turned to Joel, saying,

"Hmmm. So this is what *white* people do at their parties." Joel smiled. They
stayed a while longer and then left.

There are some moments after which you stand in a different relation to
the world. This was what happened as it began to snow a November gentle
snow in DC that night when Stokely presented us to ourselves as "other." After that I could not see myself as the norm against which all are measured. After that I became part of a group, an odd, definable gathering of white folks.
Later I would learn to define this group in an even more detailed way but for
that moment it was a group of people with the same skin color. Before this I
had heard of, spoken of, those who were black or brown as part of a group
based on skin color. Now the same had happened to me.

I began to acknowledge to myself at least that we are all "raced." This seems
especially important to remember when parents arrive in our classrooms, parents who are white and those who are not white. Each one may have differing
perceptions of us, of our race.

During my senior year at George Washington we organized a teach-in
against the war in Viet Nam. We presented a panel of speakers who discussed
the situation in many areas: Viet Nam history, sociology, and the present day
conflict. One of these experts was Bernard Fall. He was a white Jewish man,
quiet-spoken yet charismatic. He was a reporter and writer. A few weeks later
he would die reporting from Viet Nam.

The evening of the teach-in there were more African Americans on campus
than I had ever seen before. They came from Howard University, a predominantly black institution in DC, and had heard of Fall and his work. They spoke
out about the large numbers of black, Latino, and poor men who were being
drafted into the war. These men were dying in much larger percentages than
their numbers in the population. This is true even now, as I write. In Iraq, in
Afghanistan it is often working class and poor young men who are dying.

At the same time, my brother was getting worried about his draft number. While white middle class boys could be called in a universal draft, those
with "connections," doctors who would vouch for imaginative illnesses, as-
sociates who could help them in declaring their objection to war, tying up

the conscientious objector system for a while, or those who could use college deferments were able to stay out more easily. Yet the mid to late 1960s
were years when coalitions formed because the draft evened the risk to some
degree. I knew men who ended up in jail in opposition to the war or men
who ended up in Canada. Many of these were men were white.

I also knew a number of white men who died in the war. One, named Nick,
was a man I have never forgotten. He hung around with us before he left,
drank beer at a new place we had found on Pennsylvania Avenue two blocks
from the White House. After one of his many jobs, he would arrive in his
khaki shirt, blue jeans, and heavy black shoes. He would sit with his square
hands around a mug of beer and listen. One spring night he came with the
draft letter in his hand. He would not follow the advice of Maury or Bill or
Charlie—manufacture a fake heart problem, contaminate his urine, shoot off
a toe, cut off a finger, take LSD, stay up five days in a row, cry like a woman,
act crazy. Nick just smiled and drank, shook his head. He walked out, waved
without turning around, said he would come to see us when he got his leave.

But he never came back. He never walked among the tables at the student
union, never washed dishes in the kitchen of his dorm to earn money for books.
He never came back because one night somewhere in a green and steamy land
he did not own, he stumbled on a mine and his short body went sailing into the
jungle. He never came back because one dark and bird-filled night, in a land
where the "air around you moves on its knees" as he said in his letter, he stepped
on a mine and his square hands, his short fingers, went flying.

I tried to tell my father about this man and his smile, his feeling of the in-
evitability of going and even dying there, the resignation in his voice. I am not
sure my father wanted to know of this. He changed the subject immediately
when I mentioned Nick. It is so much easier to support a war in the abstract,
as my father did, in the cleanliness of theory, or in those ever-present maps
and symbols.

In 1965, in DC, we formed alliances. Black Howard students combined
with white GW students and Georgetown students to create a huge antiwar
demonstration around the White House in the spring of that year. Draft information centers, staffed by both black and white, Latino and Asian Americans, helped those who had received their draft notice figure out their options.
Neighborhood activists were also receiving more help on issues of poverty as
the war forced the more affluent and the poorer young men of draft age to

join together. This told me early on that disparate groups could join in common cause.

Trust is an edifice. We build it with dialogue, with action. Food banks in the areas where we often teach need donations. Neighborhood churches or community centers need people to volunteer one afternoon a week after school. Classes for immigrants in negotiating the English language in order to rent apartments, pay taxes, or figure out the instructions for a medical prescription need tutors.

As teachers we are in a position to join with parents of color and teachers of color to demand changes—be it a referendum for small class sizes or the demand to limit armed services recruiters' access in our lunchrooms. In St. Paul, during teacher union bargaining, the team from the union suggested having a Citizenship day so that all immigrant employees, of whom there are many, could have one day off to pursue their status as citizens.

The list of ways we can form coalitions and support each other is endless. Teachers are doing it all the time. At Roosevelt High School in Minneapolis, one year when there was conflict between African American and Somali students, female students from both these groups got together to start a Roosevelt Peace Group. It helped calm tensions. A teacher served as advisor to this group, encouraging their actions and proposals.

Reflection: Have you ever been in a situation where you felt "other"? Did this surprise you?

Suggestions: Brainstorm ways of forming coalitions with the community from which your school comes, or with city or state groups—be they working for fair labor and housing, in support of cultural events or libraries, or voting efforts. Choose one area in which to expand your involvement. Explore ways for students to form coalitions with each other.

LESSON 28: TRAUMA

In DC, I gave up attending classes regularly. I was too busy as head of our local chapter of Students for a Democratic Society (SDS), an organization that was trying to maintain alliances with black civil rights groups as some of these became more and more separated from whites. The Student Nonviolent Coordinating Committee, or SNCC, was advocating that whites now leave the civil rights action down south. The Congress on Racial Equality (CORE) was also having internal discussions about the place of whites in the movement. We whites were talking about this all the time. I was also part of organizing more antiwar activities. In Gum Springs we continued to tutor little kids in the basements of churches, worked for fair housing, and met often in the storefront office.

The result of this and the final insult to my parents was that I had to stay in DC to take another course in my political science major, and I had to get an A in it to have the right average to graduate from George Washington. I had to pay more rent and tuition and could not start a job for two more months.

My father and mother could not be reached with this news before they arrived in DC. They thought they were coming to see me walk down the aisle to receive my diploma. They were shocked and furious when they arrived to find that my graduation was not going to happen. My father went to talk with my advisor, believing he could get this decision reversed. My advisor told him there was nothing he could do.

From this vantage point, from the long, overview of my life, I see this desire and belief that I can "fix it" in me too. I still have a belief in control, in the feeling that if I just talk with someone in the right way, just present my case, just insist, I can get what I need. I believe that many of my friends who are not white know so well that there is no guarantee of such control. They know that the tide can turn, that certain words, policies, and laws can change, and all that can shift or drift away into indifference.

Harlon Dalton (1995), the black author of *Racial Healing*, relates an experience with his white wife, Jill, that illustrates the difference between these points of view. He and Jill are preparing to trespass on the lawn of a neighbor to get to the beach with a canoe. Jill does not worry about it, believes if they just explain why they are there, all will be fine. Harlon is worried, believes he "fit[s] the image of 'perpetrator' more than that of curious beachcomber." He describes his wife's reaction in this way:

> Her view of the risks associated with trespassing was not just neutral. It reflected a certain sense of entitlement, a belief that she has the right to go wherever she wants, and a confidence that she is welcome there. In other words, Jill's assessment of the situation was every bit as much shaped by her Wasp upbringing as mine was by growing up Black and male. (p. 115)

In a similar way, my father, believing he could make things right, came, tried, but the powers that be would not budge.

Many parents of students I have worked with, poor and of color, have often had to fight to get their children into advanced classes or top tracks in schools. Some of these parents have told me they have to gear up to come to schools to demand what they need for their sons or daughters And if parents feel the system, be it school, government, or medical services, is not working in their interest, their sons and daughters may feel exactly the same way.

Reflection: Do you assume if you just explain, it will work out? Why do you think others may not feel this way?

Suggestions: Include parents whenever possible in the selection of teachers and principals. Create site councils, PTAs, opportunities for parents, white and black, to get together (in separate groups if they feel this is necessary at times) at regular intervals.

LESSON 29: NARRATIVE

I have always been impatient with certain academics, with what often feels to me to be a kind of sterility of detachment from the day-to-day grittiness of words, of discussions on the run, of arguments in parent conferences, on street corners. I have a great respect, however, for the use of research when I want to make a point. I know about the necessity of statistics, theories, precedents, and scientific explanations. I would not want my doctor to tell me an anecdote about my disease or my lawyer to ignore former court rulings that relate to my case.

Yet even in these professions the place of story is important. The story the patient tells is essential to diagnosis; the lawyer tells a story in his opening and closing arguments to convince a jury, building the details of that narrative all the way through the trial. I believe that the combination of story and fact, truth and poetry, emotion and reason are what bring us understanding.

The greatest gift I inherited from my parents is my obsession to read, to know, to absorb all I can from the printed page. I love language, the way it curls around experience and, at the best times, captures it. I am grateful for those teachers who taught me and created ways for me to explore what I wanted to explore, who let me find my own way in their classes. Because of this faith in the story for itself, I go on with my own.

As my parents turned around and headed toward M Street and then out of town, on to Baltimore, New York, and home, never having seen their daughter graduate, I turned around and went toward the house to pack up and move. I was dead set on getting my A and my graduation.

I was able to get a room in the home of the minister Dick Yeo, whose United Campus Christian Ministry had allowed us to work out of his storefront on G Street the past two years. He and his wife, Ellie, had two children. I slept in a room in the attic part of the house, quiet and cut off from the family. I took an old SNCC poster along with me, and put it up on the wall near my bed—black and white civil right workers in Atlanta, Montgomery, Greeneville, marching, laughing, registering to vote, in a series of pictures on a yellow background.

June 28, 1966. I was in this attic dozing. It was afternoon, and the sun heated up my room, the small window fan barely making sleep possible. I had cramps and decided to get some rest before class. Everyone was out of the house, except me and another man who lived on the second floor. When he went out he left the back door unlocked.

A man with a knife awakened me. I have since written about this in another book. I was finally able to write about it because my friend Jill Breckinridge said, "To write it, take someone with you, go to a safe place and begin."

I took Maury to the Riverside Cafe in Minneapolis, and while he sat reading the paper, I caught the words.

I won't go into detail again, except to say, all my dearest friends all over the city were not with me that afternoon: the world went on its way. My friends were not with me as he made me walk the house, load objects into a pillowcase he had taken from my bed. No one was there as he threatened to kill me, as he laughed, as he raped me, as he pulled the sheet over my body in a gesture that puzzles me to this day. Silence.

Then, noises of the street returned: the child on her tricycle, a siren, the steady insistent beep of a truck in reverse in the alley. My hearing resumed, my life changed forever.

I have hesitated to put into any of my published work my rapist's racial identity. Years ago a black friend of mine asked me when I was about to publish my first book, *Basic Needs: A Year with Street Kids in a City School*, not to describe the rape at all. I said I could not do that. The experience was an important part of my experiences and work with young women who had been abused, raped, or beaten and who came to my classes. In that book I decided not to reveal that my rapist was black. In my next book, *A White Teacher Talks about Race*, I mention it in passing.

It *is* part of this story. It has to do with precautions, what I did to stay sane. I did not tell my parents. I knew they would want to come and take me away from those around me who could help me survive. It would also justify my father's racism, feed into his stereotypes. There were no rape crisis counseling places, no support groups then. Just me and those who gathered round, both black and white, and who did not speak of it with me unless I brought it up, but stayed vigilant.

Did this have an effect on my relationships with African Americans? I am sure it did. I had had a safe summer and school year before this one, working in places that were primarily black. Somewhere in me I had absorbed the knowledge that race was not a determiner of good or bad, right or wrong. I do not write this to excuse the rape as Eldridge Cleaver wanted to do years later in his book *Soul On Ice* with an explanation about black anger and racism. I do not write this to give a "good reason" for this rape. There is no good reason for rape, no social or sociological explanation for such violence that makes it excusable.

The consequences of this violation would last all my life, in the depression that accompanies me each day and hovers like my own shadow around my mornings and evenings. At the time I did not tell my parents what happened, and this separated me from them even further. In my fifties when I did finally tell them, just before *Basic Needs* was published, my father and mother were furious, with me, not with the man who raped me. My father questioned whether I was telling the truth. This reaction confirmed my initial instinct not to tell.

I told others. I told Jim Seymour and he understood. I told my brother and we sat in one of our old haunts among the apple trees behind my parents' tennis court and watched the sun set and did not speak.

Some students have similar stories. Nonjudgmental teachers, counselors, hall guards, educational assistants, principals, and social workers provide the opportunity for such stories to be spoken, provide the space where help comes. They do this every day. Even their students' parents may sometimes talk about events in their lives. The best educators I know are ready to listen, to find help. Yet these teachers also know they cannot take on all the responsibility that comes from the stories they hear. They know where to send students in trouble, which social worker understands Hmong culture, which counselor knows about black colleges, how to get child protection services involved immediately.

Being raped plays into stereotypes of race and fear. I find these stereotypes particularly horrible given that the rape of slave women by white slave owners was a part of the constant horror of black women's lives during that time; and not only for themselves but also for their daughters. Through my own experience I come closer to knowing what these black women might have felt. I have no idea how this affected black men at the time. For some it must have fed their anger, their sorrow, their hopelessness. For others the rape of their wives, their daughters, might have fed their motivation to fight back, to take their families and escape. I know Maury felt utterly helpless.

Being aware of rape as part of the history of the world means that this event is part of my woman narrative: a chapter in the gender story.

What happened two days later, when the cops wanted me to lie and send the wrong man to jail, is also part of the race and whiteness story. They suggested at an arraignment, after I had said that the man in court in handcuffs was not the man who raped me, that I insist that he was the man anyway.

"Getting one nigger is as good as getting any of 'em" was the way one cop put it.

Then, as now in some cities, some states, some police were aiming to arrest as many black men as they could. They were interested in wrapping up a case. An all-white jury would probably have convicted that man at the arraignment if I had followed the cops' suggestion. Black men are still being arrested in greater numbers than white men for the same crime. Men of color are most often among those who, after serving between ten and thirty years, are exonerated because DNA proves that they were wrongly convicted. This collusion between police and courts and the racism of juries, creates a system of justice that cannot be trusted by many, either blacks or whites. When our students come to us after being questioned, followed, arrested in situations while their white friends go on their way, we have to know there is a history behind this.

I believe my story of rape, and of the history of rape during slave times and after, is an important part of this book. As a white woman at least my claim was taken seriously enough to bring the cops at all, to get me checked out at a hospital and even to bring my case to an arraignment. I know that equal efforts are not always made for my black sister. Even now.

Here gender and race weave around each other in spirals of history and culture. And I know my own sorrow has nothing to do with the skin color of the man who raped me. It has everything to do with the trauma and violence done to my young body, man to woman. If a red-haired Irish American man had raped me, it would not have been any better for me. For thirty years, I would still drive, sweating at night, windows locked even in the heat of spring, toward my home. I would still find it terrifying to park in parking structures; I would still keep keys between my knuckles when I walked anywhere after dark.

When we venture into territory that is fraught with danger, both in the books we teach, the stories we hear, the ones we tell, we often find connections that are deeper than we could have imagined. At a time when women are being raped in Darfur, Sudan, at a time when they were being raped in Kosovo or Srebrenica, or Afghanistan during the reign of the Taliban, in Iraq or Jordan, and even in our own armed services, women come together in response to the continual subjugation of women in the world. Rooted in the honesty of story, we make alliances, with students, both male and female, with white and black and brown women and men, who desire to change this age-old dynamic.

Here action learning projects can happen around safety for women and children, domestic violence information, ways to counter such violence in the way we raise sons and daughters. I have watched teachers invite women who worked with young prostitutes, helping them to find a safe haven while they began a new life, to their health classes. A man from a shelter for runaway youth also visited a middle school where I taught to talk of ways young people could find hope and a place to live. There are artists and musicians too, who come to speak of or perform their work. There are doctors in clinics who are good at talking frankly with young women and young men about health concerns.

This story, the one I rarely tell, leads to more stories, more solutions, more ways of finding refuge. It comes to this: offering our students places of retreat, silence, and safety when an event, a disaster, a violation happens in their lives.

In classrooms early in the morning before the sun has risen, a quiet young woman comes when no one is there besides her teacher, and she begins to tell a story about her time in Liberia. A young boy stays after school to clean up the room and suddenly, facing away from his teacher, talks about how worried he is about his mother, who just lost her job. The best teachers offer presence, silence, and then response. Part of this job, if we do it well, includes knowing what we do not want to know.

Five months later during my wedding ceremony, real grapes, the bright idea of my mother's friend for an autumn touch, dropped off the purple corsages my bridesmaids and I held in front of us. As Dick Yeo, the minister who performed the service, asked for the rings, as he pronounced Maury and me man and wife, I could hear the soft plop, plop of each grape as it hit the wooden floor. Later, when we walked out, we could feel with each step grapes squashing underneath our satin shoes. We could smell their wine smell.

Maury's parents were standing uncomfortably with his Uncle Jack and Aunt Sylvia in front of the chapel. They told us how they thought it was a beautiful ceremony but that it was hard to concentrate because of that sound, the plopping. They did not know what it was, and then came all the squishing. They wondered if it was a Protestant thing, some ritual they had not heard about, but must respect.

A half hour later at my parents' house, the four of them, Jack and Sylvia, Mitzi and Manny Landsman, sat uneasily on damask chairs, their hands enclosing the thin stems of champagne glasses.

It wasn't until years afterward that Mitzi would tell me how they all wondered when the food would be served, of their surprise when they saw silver tureens of lobster bisque or creamed chicken and the webbed baskets of soft rolls. She said they had talked in the car, heading to the reception, about how they had heard that Protestants don't eat much, that they rarely have meals like Jews do with plenty of bread, brisket, latkes, and sour cream. Uncle Jack reassured them by saying that they could always get a sandwich later if they needed to, in the restaurant of the motel where they were staying.

It is not until now that I comprehend the gift Maury's relatives brought us that day: simply by coming to our wedding, sitting in strange rooms surrounded by antique furniture, candles, my blond sisters and brothers, and me, the *shiksa* bride.

Three weeks later, when we were married again, in a Jewish ceremony, one of Maury's uncles holding up each corner of the chuppa, my parents stayed home in Connecticut. We had this second wedding so that his parents could have a say in our mixed marriage, have some illusive control in our lives. I wore a simple wool dress and Maury, the same suit he had worn at our first wedding. Aunt Sylvia wore a red dress, and Shelley, Maury's sister, wore silver.

While I waited for this second ceremony to start, I imagined my parents walking into the fields behind the orchard, drinking cocoa on the porch warmed by the Franklin stove.

I think of it now, not because it should assume great symbolic weight. I think of this because it reminds me of how much it takes for each of us to come out of the safe rooms of our past, our present, out of the small kitchens, the places where sickness was steamed away, where chicken cooked, to come out of our book-lined homes into a place called *other*. It is one of the things they refused to do, to go out of that place, to be part of a ceremony they did not understand. I was in the place of discomfort that Dr. Joseph White talks about, and as Maury's parents were when they ventured into Wasp territory. I do not remember why they decided to stay home. I know my father was angry that this second wedding was happening at all. I know he still had grave doubts about me marrying a Jew. Neither of them ever asked how it went.

There is something I wish I had said to my father, when he worried aloud about me marrying outside any religion, something I wanted to say to a woman who said to me, the night before my first wedding, that she had thought of marrying a Jew, just to spite her parents: I wish I had said to him, to her, that love doesn't happen that way. Rather it happens by chance. There is a voice that sings and we like that voice or maybe the sex is good at first and love follows. It just happened that I decided to stay in Maury's rooms for a while one spring in DC and then stayed even longer, despite the small mice that inhabited his oven, the smell of cabbage from the apartment nearby. We cannot plan our weddings, know who will attend them, who will stand and shift feet nervously as we marry. These moments of love, of celebration happen finally, if the weather is right, the grapes are ripe, our aunt is healthy and makes the trip.

I would have said to my father that I think changing the world will happen by chance too. We can work, walk the lines in the cold, hold out our arms and our handmade signs to the universe. We can do the task of organizing all our life, and yet be left with a deep appreciation of luck.

If as teachers we account for this, for the way luck plays a part in our work lives, our neighborhood lives, perhaps we will be much more relaxed about our failures. This does not mean we stop organizing in shelters or holding poetry slams in the library. It does mean that when all our best plans fail—parents don't show up in a snowstorm or a play-off game competes with our crucial meeting—we simply go back and start again without heaping blame on ourselves.

At this second wedding, I also felt an exhilaration I did not feel at the first. I now know that what made our second wedding so different from the first had to do with revelation, with reticence not required. It had to do simply with the fact that Aunt Sylvia in the red dress, that Manny, Mitzi, and Shelley and the other relatives who came and planted lipstick tattoos on my cheek, all knew I had been raped just months before. At my first wedding, I was Miss New England reserve. I kept myself tight. I was satin heavy and silent, and except for my college friends there who knew, living with a secret from so many present.

At this second wedding, all was known and *life went on.* It was terribly important for me to know that life would go on, that Aunt Flo would speak in her high, Baltimore voice about where we were going to live; that Manny, Maury's father, would make the invitations by hand because he loved to do calligraphy. It was important that five different relatives at different times would hold my hand longer than usual, would explain to me the chuppa, the broken glass, and their significance, again and again.

I was being immersed. Just as I say today that we need all kinds of experiences—the conceptual, the dialogue, and the immersion—this last is the way I was led into understanding the culture and even the religion of my husband.

Students need such acceptance and understanding. In my in-laws' home, while they were not thrilled that I was breaking up the Jewish family, they did not make me feel ashamed. Also, because they had lived lives that involved violence at times or combativeness, or awareness of their fragile history as Jews, they were able to absorb my story, without melodrama, without judgment.

There is a basic openness that is at the crux of good teaching, good educating. It is the knowledge that a new immigrant group may arrive without warning and enter our classes by chance, having chosen the certain neighborhood where we teach as their home. And so we will find ourselves wondering about the country from which these children came, the music and words in their lives, the contour of the land. When Hmong students entered my teaching world I remember my colleagues studying a map of Laos and Thailand, wondering how it would be for kids, their parents, living in such a cold climate. When these students took over a playing field for soccer after school and the Native American kids were angry because they wanted the same place for their football games, it took fumbling, mistakes, and added police officers until we found translators, went to community meetings, and worked out a sports schedule. We can't know, even in an all-white school, what personalities will assemble in our third hour by the chance of scheduling.

To be open to this uncertainty, and somewhat humble before it, may be what fine teachers possess more than anything else.

> *Reflection:* Think of a time in your life when you were traumatized. What was your initial reaction? Did this change? Think of a time when a student came to you with a story that was hard to hear. What did you do? Have you ever had an experience of being truly immersed in a culture that was not the one you were raised in? What part has luck or chance played in your teaching, in your life?

> *Suggestions:* Create a woman's book group, discussion group. Explore same sex math classes. Brainstorm ways to reach both young men and young women in order to break cycles of failure or lack of confidence.

> When a new immigrant group moves into your school district, explore with city and state workers what those students will need when they arrive at your school door. Find articles for all teachers and staff to read about this group, keeping in mind the danger of stereotyping or limiting expectations.

6

Working Within, Working from the Outside

LESSON 30: TRIBALISM, TRANSLATION

I took a job at Yale University, which lasted about nine months. I was in charge of punching in data on cards for the computer center down the block from the Yale office. It was tedious work, in great heat and odor, some students having slept on couches in the center when they were into some important research, going unwashed for days. And I am not sure what it was for. I am not sure what I was counting, although I do remember something about telephone poles in Togo.

Every day I would meet Maury for lunch at Commons on the Yale campus. Every day we would eat with his friends, including Andreas Eshete, a man from Ethiopia, who wore his hair in a "natural." Andreas would later go back to his home country and risk his life in secret political activity. I remember that walking down the streets of New Haven with him, some young African American men with straightened hair would stop, look at his head, an aura of black curls around his fine boned face, and ask him how he did it that way, how it came out like that. I remember wondering if Andreas ever got tired of being an object of curiosity. A year later he would laugh at how the styles changed in the United States and how the kids now went by him, saying "cool Afro" and how he wanted to say he was from Africa, this was how he had always worn it.

Aside from Andreas there were few blacks in my life. Until I finally quit my
Yale job, I had little to do with the African American community in New
Haven, except in street greeting, or interaction at the Laundromat around the
corner.

Is it so natural in us, the tribal? Is it a *human* inheritance: the desire to stay
with those who look, pray, sound like we do? Of course the flip side to this
clannishness is exclusion. And even more dramatically, war and terror. It
might be that in the alliances that form as we love, work, and sometimes live
together, that we break down the very nature of tribalism without losing our
cultural identities.

My next job was as an assistance worker for the New Haven Department of
Social Services. I was to process applications, determine eligibility, and pay
visits to verify continued compliance with the rules of the welfare system in
that city. This was 1967.

There I am standing in the apartment in a housing project, having just
parked the black sedan with the county seal on it, on the street nearby. There
she was, her hair in a net pulled tight at the nape of her brown neck, her eyes
darting around the kitchen, angry, anxious. I waited for her anger to soften for
a moment before I tried to speak. How little I knew. All Sheila wanted was a
phone in her place. She was asthmatic and had three children who sometimes
had health emergencies. All she wanted was the paper that said welfare would
pay. There I was, another white woman with power in my twenty-two-year-
old hands. She had raised a son who was in high school, and now had two little ones at her knees, pulling on her apron, crying quietly. Suddenly she
collapsed on a chair across from me. I pulled up a chair facing her.

We talked, one toddler on her lap leaning back to look up at her face,
touching her cheek with his small fingers, the other four-year-old girl staring
at me in my sundress and sandals. Sheila told me about her oldest, on his way
to graduation. I said very little and yet we found ourselves laughing at one
point. I cannot remember what we laughed at, just that we were both surprised. I handed her the form to sign for the phone, the place for the doctor's
signature circled with a red pen. I promised to come back for the completed
form in a week.

I walked out her door, never having done what I was supposed to do according to the rules of the welfare policy: look under the bed for a man's
shoes, look in closets for his clothes, just in case she was getting supplemental

income from the babies' father. She could be immediately disqualified from any state help if this was so.

When I returned to the car, there was a small gathering of black and white women and young children waiting for me. They handed requests, in awkward printing, in elegant cursive, or on official forms, for telephones, clothing vouchers, or medical assistance. I held one of the babies while her mother reached into her pocketbook for a slip that was signed by her doctor. I remember the baby felt warm in my arms. I remember the women's voices rising as they explained how difficult it was to get a job without a telephone.

Soon I would go back to my office and I would hear some workers complain about "these people." Always the race of the women was mentioned, the use of the word "nigger" frequent in the conversations I heard in the back of the room where the eligibility clerks sat. The entire staff of workers, clerks, and supervisors was white.

A day or two later I found that almost all requests for phones were turned down.

Around this time there were rebellions in the streets of many cities, including New Haven. Social workers, case workers, and supervisors were told to order all field workers like me to look in refrigerators for food when we went on home visits, asked to report any new bicycles or objects that looked like they may have been taken in the two days of looting and burning that had occurred in New Haven. One man, Joe, who had worked at the welfare agency for a year, refused, saying he would not take food from his poor clients. The supervisor, Mrs. Harding, said that he could not go out, and would have to switch to a paperwork job. Joe stood up, letting the chair clatter behind him as it hit the floor. He left his ID on the table and walked away. He never came back. I admired him then. And I stayed. I never looked in a refrigerator. I stepped over an occasional shiny tricycle and never reported it. Yet, I was haunted by Joe's clear, decisive act, his quiet dignity.

Every section of the welfare building felt demeaning to me in different ways. The section where white men sat and worked on federal forms was in the back of the long, many-windowed factory-like room where we caseworkers sat at desks lined up in an open space. Whenever I went back there, to ask a question or leave off a form, the men stopped talking and simply watched. Some made comments about my long legs, others about my hair, a few about my young looking face. Some even reached toward a female caseworker's breasts or buttocks as she walked by.

I can smell cigar, hear their comments. I can feel my skin crawl and illogical shame creeping into my face with its unbidden flush. I blamed myself, what I wore, how I smelled. I worried I attracted attention because I laughed with colleagues back on the other side of the room. These men triggered in me a wild fear. I would go home at night furious.

Because I wanted to keep my job I learned to swerve quickly out of the way, or whose desk to avoid walking by altogether. I went back there less and less. Finally, a sympathetic male caseworker collected my forms and took them back with his own.

Another image comes back: the tiny offices where clients had to meet with workers in order to submit their initial application for welfare. They were put through the indignity of answering personal questions while everyone in the waiting room could hear their responses. The woman who worked as a receptionist yelled at those who came, demanding to know if they "couldn't for Chrissakes find a job!"

Reflecting back on these days in New Haven has let me experience again that feeling, the fury at the end of a work day, the illogical self-blame I experienced each time a man reached out his arm toward my waist. Remembering this is to begin to understand the parents of some of the students who come before me, black and white, in their frustration and anger. After six months I had to decide whether to stay or go.

Each of us will probably find ourselves in such a situation. Do we stay in an oppressive system and hope to change it from within, or do we leave it, make a statement with our bodies, and look for places where we can act on our beliefs?

As teachers we deal with this decision all the time. We are all needed in a democracy: the one who walks away and protests from the outside and the one who stays and fights the system on the job. We need the woman who gives up the fight for gender equity because the daily emotional cost is too much and the one who goes to court, who stays for the years it takes to pursue a gender equity lawsuit like the one involving the mines in Minnesota as depicted in the movie *North Country*. In each instance there are times we can cross tribal lines, form alliances.

One high school in my state had a beautiful door that welcomed students each day and was located across from the parking lot where students who drove to school parked their cars. The door that was used by students who were poor, often of color, and thus came by bus, was ramshackle and dirty, graffiti covered and surrounded by trash and had no landscaping. Teachers began to listen more closely to students and noticed that they were very aware of these two different entryways. Finally, through work on the teachers' part and a positive response from the principal along with student effort, a new door was constructed for the students who rode the bus. It made all the difference in the start of their day. Now the teachers and administration are working on the city to put in a bus shelter for students who wait for their bus in the freezing cold Minnesota winter.

Other friends I know are starting up new charter schools, are working outside the regular public school system to create ways of educating students without the bureaucracy of large districts. They are important in their creativity, in their decision to try something new. There is room for all of us now.

I finally left the welfare job because I could not be part of what a system like this insisted I do. I also worked for the most disagreeable supervisor. She questioned every phone, every addition of income for medicine and every service I requested for my clients, often referring to these women and children by the n-word. There were always openings in her cadre of workers, as a result of the round-robin of us who left after four months or so. She was never fired.

Reflection: Why do you believe we stay in enclaves, live with those who look like us? Has there been a time in your life when you crossed this line? Have you ever left a job, a school system in protest?

Suggestion: Create a school theme, lesson plan, or a unit topic around the idea of Insiders and Outsiders. Bring in historical examples of those inside and outside the system who worked for change.

LESSON 31: BOUNDARIES

In my next job at a library center on Congress Avenue I served mostly black children in the after-school hours. The library provided them with books and art materials, classes in story writing and poetry. The building was one of those old brick ones with long arched windows and lots of interior woodwork. The shelves were oak and glowed with the softening light of age and varnish.

I loved this work, loved the quiet mornings when a few elders would come to sit and read the paper or a novel. I loved the family of boys whose names all ended with "ell"—Darnell, Idell, Rodell—and the odd name out, Mathew. I loved to watch as Idell outran the social worker who was trying to get him into school, darting in and out of the alleys he knew with the soles of his feet, instinctively doubling back and appearing, three blocks later looking over his shoulder. I did not like that he was not in school, that he did not have proof of inoculations, did not know how to read, being in second grade; but what I admired, despite my concern, was his intelligence, his ability to outwit adults who eventually "captured" him and brought him to the doctor or to school.

In the late afternoons, Idell would come in to look at books, sitting on the carpeted floor, turning over each page slowly, savoring the colors, the words. If I were free I would read to him, circling him with one arm. He would lean against me, sometimes even falling asleep.

Once he woke up, looked at me and said, "Miss Julie, you read real nice. I had a good ol' dream when you read to me." And then he drifted off. I was able to put a pillow under his head, curl him up in a safe corner, and he slept there until 4 p.m. when his mother came to get him after work.

Other days his brothers raced around the room, climbing into the sunlight streaming into the bay windows, dancing on ledges, jumping down, and grabbing pencils from the front desk, darting out of the room with their treasure. Bryna, the other worker, and I tried to find ways to keep them somewhat quiet, without stifling their joy. We rewarded them for going to school, offering pencils and paper if they brought us notes from their teachers.

Part of my job was to walk out into the neighborhood to tell stories in surrounding elementary classrooms. With my sack of books I was welcomed into schools, where for fifteen minutes I read to the rapt attention of twenty first and second graders. These children were white and African American. I memorized the texts so the books faced outward and students could follow each picture as the stories spun into the room. I remember the upturned faces of the children. It was here I began to fall in love with schools, with their smell and their noise and their pulse. It was here that I began to develop the excitement and comfort I still feel when I walk into a school building.

I began to notice the way the little ones turned their faces to stare at my face, my smile, my mouth, rather than at the pages turning before their eyes. It was me, in my ability to read and speak and laugh that they were interested. Many elementary teachers have told me since that they experience this as well: kids are often more fascinated by the real live person in their midst than the printed page itself. Since these youngsters were just learning to read they were especially enthralled with adults who could do this task that felt so difficult to them. And to have a visitor read to them was especially interesting. This bodes well for bringing volunteers into our buildings every day, every hour to read to students. And especially when these volunteers look like them, speak like them.

Thirty years later, as a poet in the schools, I would find myself working with third graders again, one of whom was named Alan. He had been seriously abused most of his life. Each week I would arrive, set up my activity for the hour, and Alan would walk up slowly, climb into my lap and sit there as I taught. The teacher, whom I greatly respected, nodded his okay, and we both went through the year, holding him, letting him go when he was ready and then letting him rest against us when he needed to come back.

I was stunned by the way physical contact settled Alan down, by the way he stopped running around the room when Josh put a hand on his shoulder, or by the way he began to spell words he wanted to use when either Josh or I pulled a chair up across from him, our knees almost touching his. This was a basic physical connection. Alan was under the care of child protection agencies, in and out of homes, and even sent back to his father until new abuse occurred and they took him out again. There was no way to let this go—no way to keep him out of our thoughts, our anxiety, our dreams. In this work with young, vulnerable children especially, we struggle with boundaries, with how to keep our center, our sense of ourselves as separate people, intact.

I have finally come to accept that it is part of the job to connect emotionally with students, with their joy and sorrow. And how we cope with this, when we feel helpless or frustrated is something we figure out gradually over the years. We may work out, run, paint, or raise dogs, farm a garden plot or watch science fiction. We may also become advocates: calling protection services, writing letters, running for school board or legislative office. The desire to do something, to fight for children is one of our finest desires.

And in the process of working this out we may find ourselves romanticizing street kids. For a while I had to keep reminding myself that city kids, poor kids, even kids in prison are like kids all over the world: they respond to attention, respect, understanding, and limit setting. Simplistic or condescending solutions geared toward certain groups of kids based on their race or culture can be dangerous. I have seen teachers come back from a training about kids in poverty by Ruby Payne for instance stating, "Oh. Now I know why they can't learn. Those poor kids." I have had teachers tell me that African American students can only work with strict authority in the classroom and don't respond to my type of personality. We have to watch for that tricky line where awareness leads to generalization, where knowledge of culture leads to overreaching assumptions, losing the individuality of each student within his or her cultural or economic background.

I search for pity, condescension, racism that must have been a part of me in my work at the library center. I know they were there. I want to give you scenes or dialogue. I cannot. I might have buried them, ashamed. I do remember coming home, finally believing I was doing meaningful work.

Reflection: Has there ever been a time in your life when you lost your boundaries, your sense of yourself, and your family apart from your job? How did you cope with it? What are some generalizations about poor students or students of color or students from certain cultural groups that you have been taught? Has anyone taught you about white kids or wealthy kids and how they behave generally?

Suggestions: Create a class character with your students. Encourage them to imagine this character's likes, dislikes, background, job, house. Continue by having them describe this character in different situations. Encourage them to make him do unexpected things, unusual things given her race or culture.

Set up ways with teachers in your school or district to separate yourselves from your jobs. Start an after-school yoga class, a volleyball team, a chance to meditate or relax together.

LESSON 32: INTUITION, CRAFT

About this time I was asked if I was interested in working at a teen center in the same area of the city two nights a week. I said I would like to do that and arrived at the center one dark night in the fall of 1967, notebook in hand. It was noisy, with a lounge where kids hung out and talked, danced, and joked together. In the back, in a bare room with fluorescent lighting and bleak walls, there was a long table and paper and pencils. There was a group of young people who wanted to write a play and I was sent to help them get it off the ground. Six or seven young men had signed up to write and produce. They were all black between the ages of seventeen and twenty.

I know I felt conspicuous in my otherness. Yet I did not feel hostility directed toward me because I was white. After all, Martin Luther King was still alive. Integration was a stated goal for many.

It took some time to build trust in this new setting, this new neighborhood. Twice a week we worked on a script, the young men coming in on some scheduled nights, disappearing on others. This was preparing me for the nomadic students I would work with later, who moved from home to home, street to street, and showed up for class when they could. The most consistent young man in this group was Melvin, slim, light skinned, and sweet. He was serious about the play, refused to discuss anything about his life, but was willing to tape dialogue into a recorder for me to develop as the basic script. By the time we were done with the first two acts I had lined up a theater space for the final performance.

The play was about drugs, dealing, and redemption. I do believe the redemption was part real, and part hope. I was not as naive as I sound here. I did take note when one or another of my students nodded off or slurred his speech, smiling at me in a helpless way. I was not ignorant of the signs of heroin slowness or pot-inspired happiness.

During this time I was hospitalized for an appendectomy. Melvin and his friends came in boots, hairnets, and leather jackets to visit. As they glanced around at the older white men and women with whom I shared a room, each of these patients pulled back into their beds. My visitors smiled, handed me a box of candy, told me to get well and come back soon. We talked about the script, the theater, what was happening at the center. A few minutes after they left my father walked in to see me, curious about the young black men who had passed him on the way out. I smiled and said they were my students at the teen center. He changed the subject.

By the time spring rolled around and I was out of recovery, I went back to my job full time to discover that the library where I had been working had cut back on personnel. I was assigned to a different center, one next door to where I lived. Melvin was in jail. And, as it turned out, he had been the glue that held the play together. The others drifted off, came back once in a while, then disappeared entirely. For a while I showed up at the center every week just in case.

Eventually, my boss pulled me off that work. She said she wanted me to focus on the new library on Chapel Street.

I have been a teacher long enough to understand that I might have had more of an effect on these playwrights than I ever will know. I have had young men and women come to me years after I taught them in middle school to tell me how important a class was, how, when I asked them take attendance or distribute books, I made them feel worthwhile. At the time I might have assigned them these tasks because I was at a loss about how to reach them. I might have done it to keep them quiet for a while so others could work. Many teachers tell me stories of those students who stop in, years later, after school one day to talk about their lives. These former students surprise teachers with their gratitude, with what they remember of their classes.

A student whom I will call Jamal was defiant, obstreperous, and difficult in class. He came from a black family dubbed a "problem family" in the lounge, in the main office, in the classroom. One day Jamal threatened his teacher, whom I will call Tony. Jamal swore and stomped out of class. Tony, a white man, called the office and reported the incident. He arranged to meet with Jamal and the principal after classes that day. Jamal became sullen, rarely looking Tony in the eye. The principal asked Tony what he needed from Jamal to allow him to return to class. At this point the teacher looked directly into his student's eyes and said, "I need Jamal to be in my class for gifted students. He is too smart for the class he has been assigned to now." Jamal's response was electric. Jamal will tell you now that it changed his life. He came to the more advanced class, and with the help and support of his teacher, parents, and community, began to take school seriously.

We do things instinctively. The part that intuition plays in how we teach is immeasurable. There are some young teachers I have met who seem to be born to the job of teaching in an urban school. There are others who have to work harder at it. Eventually though, the way we interact with students becomes more and more automatic and authentic, a part of who we are.

Ultimately we will never know all of the ways we affect our students' lives. I did not know this at the time of the play and felt a failure when the final performance did not come to fruition. Wise mentors have reminded me all through my career that I will never know the effect I am having. These principals, fellow teachers were essential in encouraging me to stay on the job.

Reflection: Describe a time you were surprised to learn of your own success in reaching an unlikely student.

Suggestions: Form a support group for new teachers in your building. Become an unofficial mentor for a new teacher whom you admire and want to help navigate the profession.

LESSON 33: PERCEPTION

On April 4, 1968, Martin Luther King Jr. was assassinated. I heard the news as I walked out of work. Maury arrived home early that day. We were glued to the TV. We did not know about the circumstances, about James Earl Ray, about FBI surveillance of King. And we only vaguely sensed the cosmic shift that would come to this country as a result of the assassination. We did not know yet how the riots would follow, leaving Maury's father's liquor store untouched because Manny Landsman hired blacks, how cities would burn out of rage and grief.

The previous spring, when King took his power and turned it against the war, and when he and Malcolm X became reconciled, I had begun to see how powerful he was becoming. And now, in my most despairing moments, I believe that his death was because of this very power. That Malcolm's death also came when it did as he reached out toward those of us in white America who worked for civil rights and toward compromise, makes me wonder who orchestrated these deaths. The alliance of these two men must have frightened many in power at the time, either within the Black Muslim organization or within the white power structure. When we worked together in small numbers, in individual communities, perhaps we were not seen as a threat. But when blacks in great numbers, joined with whites in large numbers, fear of the power of this alliance must have kicked in somewhere. Is this paranoia unfounded? I am not sure.

I am also not sure that, even with all my work in civil rights, I took in the death of King with the same intensity as my black counterparts. I believe this has to do with the fact that the death of King would not affect my children's future in this world as deeply as it might affect the black children who lose out when such a powerful black leader dies. I know black friends who were in their twenties at the time have told me that on the day King died they felt more anger and more hopelessness than they had ever felt before.

I think this is true about events today, in all areas of our city. When crack cocaine is dealt and used in the cities among those of color and is given a greater punishment than straight cocaine used in the suburbs, whites may not perceive this as racist. When voting machines break down in black areas of Miami, many might not see this as intentional or a result of neglect of the rights of those of color. When the faces of black suspects are pictured on the news or in the paper, and whites are only named, many will miss this disparity. Even now we may literally see things differently

And so in schools we might be seeing things, *perceiving* things differently from our black colleagues, from our students, and from their parents.

My ingrained sense of hope did not change after King died. At the same time, his death seemed to signal, that no matter how powerful you get, no matter your Nobel peace prize, your time with presidents and rulers of the world, if you are black you can still be taken down at the whim of white men. And if, as in the case of Robert Kennedy or John Kennedy, you earned some trust from black men and women, you, a white man, were also at risk.

Ben Mchie, founder of the African American Registry told me, when I asked him about the affect of King's death:

> Dr. King's murder sent a message of defiance to all Americans of African descent in a way that frightens our community to this day. The killing brought the word martyr vividly close to everyone, saying, *this will happen if you challenge the status quo.*

Carolyn Holbrook, a professor at Hamline University and coordinator for the Givens Foundation of Black Literature at the University of Minnesota, also responded to my question about King's death in an e-mail:

> African Americans are never relieved of the grief we suffered as a result of the legacy of slavery. That grief is as much a part of us as our skin, our bones and the blood that courses through our veins. Martin Luther King was, in many ways, an archetype for us, an exemplar whose power and courage gave us hope that we could overcome 2nd class citizenship one day and finally be counted as full fledged Americans. That hope was immediately dashed with his shocking assassination. White people, even well-meaning white people who grieved his death, could never experience his death in the same way.

Pam Booker, integration specialist for a multidistrict school program wrote to me:

I think there was a lot of rage and anger about the *way* Dr. King lost his life. I also think it was like losing a family member, a father, a brother, a son because he was exposing the reality of African Americans and others on a national and international scale. It was the loss of leadership and voice for the Black community that was silenced and the message really has not been as passionate and heartfelt since.

I did experience fear after King died. I cannot articulate where this originated, except to say that I know I wanted his nonviolent approach to succeed, and that without him, I worried what the consequences might be for our country if we abandoned his approach.

By the spring of 1968, we were planning on leaving for Northfield, Minnesota, where Maury would be teaching philosophy at Carleton College. We had no idea it would be a lifetime residency in this northwestern state. We were to be there so Maury could fill in for a professor on leave for one year. I was not sorry to go. I would miss the kids in the library center, our friends in graduate school. I would even miss the occasional Sunday afternoons at my parents' home overlooking the hill. They had not pressured us to come out more than we wanted, and I felt gratitude for this. They were engaged in a struggle with Lesley at the time, angry at her relationship with Bill Lee, a black man she was dating in Boston, and waiting for my brother Mark to begin his rebellion. I was becoming, in comparison, their "good" daughter. After all, Maury was at least "off-white." I had also become pregnant, which was exactly what we had hoped for when we began trying two months before. This, the arrival of a first grandchild also endeared Maury to my family and me to his.

As we pulled out of my parents' driveway to begin the summer trip to Minnesota, I was ready for the baby, the new state, the distance from DC. I was not aware yet that trauma sears itself into our bodies, changes the electricity of our nerve pathways, our brain structure permanently. I left the apple trees and blond fields of Connecticut believing I had fully recovered. And in a sense this was true. But still accompanying me was the knife light, the odd sweaty-palmed fear of being alone on certain days.

To respect trauma on a personal and historical level is one way of coming to terms with its persistence. This is also true for the students we are seeing who have lived through personal trauma in their home country different from our own. Respecting the time it takes to heal is the beginning of reconciliation, redemption.

In my last year of teaching at a middle school in Minneapolis, I allowed students to visit my room with their lunch. Sothol, a Cambodian student, would come in, get out the chessboard, and play. Sometimes I would be his opponent, other times it would be his friend. In either case, in the quiet I insisted upon when students arrived at my door sandwiches in hand, Sothol would begin to tell me about his life, how worried he was about his sister who had to do all the cooking and could not get her homework done. I learned about his neighborhood, his response to the events in the Cambodian community. I learned about the trauma many from his country had experienced. All around me in this school, teachers were creating this kind of time for their students.

Reflection: Where were you when Martin Luther King Jr. was shot? Were you alive? How old were you? Do you remember the effect this had on you?

Suggestions: Create new and original ways to recognize King's birthday. Think about reconciliation hearings, art projects, murals, action learning units. Work on activist solutions with students as early as grade four to change what Dr. King would have wanted changed.

7

Gender, Race, and Separation

LESSON 34: SEPARATISM

Last year I taught education courses at Carleton College, thirty years after we had left Northfield and Maury's career as a philosophy professor. Sitting in my office, overlooking the center of campus with its soft green that glowed in leaves of lime yellow and hesitant dark undergrowth, I found myself uncomfortable. This surprised me. Yes, the drive from the cities was a hassle, and yes, I had not been to the campus in a few years, the last time being when I filled in for a professor on leave. Yet I liked Carleton students and had friends on campus from our days when Maury taught here.

From my sheltered office window, ornate and tucked into the corner of a building, I watched a couple doing tai chi under a tree, a young white man with dreads laughing as he talked into a cell phone, his white t-shirt catching the light. As I waited for my afternoon class, I felt again the frustration and anxiety I experienced so long ago when we came to Northfield.

My arrival in Northfield in 1968 began a five-year pause in the rhythm of work and traffic, neighborhood and curving back alley. When Maury and I first moved to Northfield in 1968 we were in our mid-twenties. After a summer of camping out of our VW bug, and me growing bigger and more rounded with my baby, we arrived in town. Around this time the Koerner Commission came out with the famous quote: "Our nation is moving toward two societies, one black, one white, separate and unequal" (as cited in *People's Chronology*, New York 1992, p. 1015).

In Northfield, Minnesota, there are two colleges on either side of the main highway, St. Olaf and Carleton. Carleton is supposed to be more like an eastern, Ivy League school, the "Harvard of the Midwest." St. Olaf was described as the Midwest school, Lutheran, local, not so cosmopolitan. At that time the sign on the entryway to the town read: "Northfield, Home of Cows, Colleges and Contentment."

On our second night there, we attended a dinner for new faculty members. The TV was on, showing cops rioting at the 1968 Democratic convention. We watched as a friend from Yale, Roger Dexter, turned toward the screen, blood running from a wound in his head. I was struck by his fierce smile. We had planned to go to this convention until my pregnancy. I could not risk losing my child. But our friends were there. Just as the cameras shifted back to Dan Rather, trying to get onto the floor to report what he was seeing outside the center, our hostess flipped off the set.

Over dinner we listened as those around the table talked of their desire to put a bubble around Northfield. They wanted to keep it safe, educated, crime free, and peaceful, almost pristine. I remember stopping midbite, my fork part way to my mouth, and turning to Maury who looked just as uncomfortable as I did. I know I asked about the election, about concerns in the town for the Viet Nam war, about issues on campus. There was some discussion of the Democratic Party in Minnesota, about politics in town, about the split between McCarthy supporters and Humphrey supporters. Many of those around the table were Democrats. Yet that evening I felt disconnected from them, aware of a divide, not sure what it was exactly.

Do parents strive for a version of the bubble in our schools today? Do we see the effort to keep certain school buildings, certain programs white, surrounded by programs that get fewer resources, and who serve Native Americans or blacks, part of the striving for the bubble? When whites do it, trying to keep their schools tracked, providing AP courses for their own, we accept this as wanting what is best for their children. When blacks want their own schools, when they want black academies, or Native Americans want Native schools, we see this as separatist and segregationist. Often white parents want to define what gifted means, and then claim entrance for their own based on European requirements.

And without the power of resources, without equal access to money and facilities because of systemic discrimination and the problematic way schools are funded according to property tax levies, there is a danger in any version of segregated education. A history of discrimination and poverty means many schools for students of color do not have the money to provide their version of an elitist education for their kids. In wealthy areas of the cities or in certain suburban districts, parents are now raising money themselves to fund arts, extra teachers, and technology: just a few of the things money can buy.

I have concern about bubbles of any kind because the lack of students of differing nationalities or cultures in any setting denies all the presence of culture and color and a global education. When we include students in our schools, our programs, whose home language is not English we are benefiting the white students all around them. When we invite young Muslim women to join book groups with European American and African American women, when we integrate our theater programs naturally with Latino boys, with Laotian girls, the benefits for white students, who will soon have Latino, Asian, and Indian bosses and colleagues, are obvious. I am concerned then, with the presence of schools based on nationality or culture as well as white programs that segregate.

At the same time it is understandable that parents of color who sense that their sons and daughters are being taught by primarily white teachers who do not expect their children to achieve would want their own programs. It seems logical that they would push for a setting that would challenge their sons and daughters and respect their community. If this means demanding a charter school for African American students, or a Native school, this may be the answer. In Minnesota some school systems have figured this out in less separate ways: students may go to Afrocentric Academy in the afternoons after attending their home school in the mornings, or Hmong students may work in a Hmong center for part of the day and attend integrated classrooms the rest of the time. The ways of doing this are only limited by the imaginations of those who work in our educational system.

While studies show that students of color often do well in integrated schools, they do not always stay in those schools if they are sent away from their neighborhood. The power and pull of being home in their community is strong. The history of discrimination that ultimately caused a lack of black teachers in our national educational system is important to keep in mind here too. When *Brown vs. Board of Education* was decided and schools suddenly integrated, we lost some of the most gifted educators of African American children:

> With desegregation came massive layoffs and demotions: Approximately 38,000 African Americans teachers and administrators in 17 states lost their positions between 1954 and 1965 (Holmes, 1990; King, 1993). These numbers do not tell

the full story that these layoffs and demotions had on some Black communities. Foster (1997) explains that according to U.S. census data at the turn of the 20th century, the number of Black teachers had risen close to 70,000—close to half of the Black professional population at the time. She suggests that between 1932 and 1948 the number of Black teachers doubled. Thus, as the Black population grew throughout the South, as well as the North and Midwest, so did the Black teaching population. Yet, to consider the fact that close to a third of these teachers lost their teaching positions after the Brown decision tells a grim story. Some would argue that this marked the beginning of the troubled cycle of underachievement for many African American students and that their quality of education has not been the same since. (Milner and Howard, 2004)

Recently I have been reading about primarily poor, primarily black neighborhood schools making unusual gains in educating their students. The Knowledge is Power Program (KIPP) schools springing up all over the country, the Geoffrey Canada school in the South Bronx, and many others developed by Haitian, Jamaican, and African American educators are doing well. One key component to these gains has been parental support and participation. It is clear there are ways to meet the needs of students in any educational context. Perhaps it takes abandoning insistence on one way as the right way. It takes looking at separation as a complex reaction to historical losses and present practices. It also takes acknowledging that whites too have been pushing to create their own culturally identified schools, yet have not named them as such.

For our first year in Northfield, we lived in the house of a professor on leave, surrounded by African masks from trips to many continents. I took a class from a visiting professor, Roger Abrahams, on African and African American folktales. In Roger's class I was struck by the beauty of story, the intricacy of drums as a way to tell the news, the way culture survives and adapts despite its erasure from the institutions of a larger society.

After taking this course, it struck me again how arbitrary and how slanted is the designated history, music, literature, and art that we teach. Who chooses how many pages to spend on slavery, on black culture, on the Underground Railroad, on messages in quilts, versus battles or Confederate culture or economics?

That first year we lived next door to Mary and Fred Easter, a black couple. Fred was brought in to recruit black students for Carleton and to advise a program called A Better Chance or ABC. This program brought kids of color from city high schools to Northfield High and then counseled them into college. Mary was a dancer raising two small children, trying to get to dance classes in Minneapolis, an hour away. After Aaron was born she brought me food, stopped by to talk, invited us over for dinner. I am not sure what kind of impact it had on me or how relevant it was to our friendship that Mary was black. I do know that being able to talk with her I felt a familiarity that united us. She was from Virginia and had gone to boarding school and college in New York. Fred grew up in Harlem. Most of the time Mary and I talked about children and life in a small town and music and love. We have remained friends for forty years. Then, being with her was being with my odd combination of New England propriety, integration work, and leftist politics.

And even when Fred Hampton was shot in Chicago a year later, when Eldridge Cleaver's book *Soul On Ice* had become a best seller, when black Jackson State students were killed in their dormitory two years after that I am not sure what we said to each other about these things. Yet I do remember late, late into the night, after bottles of wine and good food, the four of us left at the party, Aaron asleep on the Easters' bed upstairs, Fred would talk about what he believed, what he feared in the United States. We listened.

During these same years on Carleton's campus, black students became more outspoken and honest. Mark Boreli and Velma Neal introduced us to Coltrane's *A Love Supreme*, an album I had not heard, even though I had listened to Coltrane's drummer, Elvin Jones, at the Village Vanguard a few years before. We spent considerable time with black students, in our living room, in others' apartments on campus, at meetings, and at anti–Viet Nam war rallies. Our babysitters were white and black. While there was a move toward separate places of identity and retreat (Governor George Wallace was defying integration, blocking the schoolroom doors in Alabama), there were also times when people came together.

From 1968 to 1973, the war in Viet Nam was continuing to tear middle class families apart as their sons were drafted along with the poor kids, both white and of color. Students were shot dead by National Guard soldiers at Kent State while peacefully protesting the war, and at Carleton, Maury burned his draft card, while some white students headed to jail for refusing to go to Viet Nam. During this time, the Supreme Court upheld busing to achieve integration in schools.

Reflection: What are advantages to integrated schools? What are advantages to busing for integration? What are advantages to separate academies? How do you reconcile the two?

Suggestions: Think of ways within your school system to create oases of support and safety for cultural groups. These could include once-a-week meetings, half days of immersion in their culture, whole days in separate settings with exchanges built in. What would fit your district?

Look at the sidebar for items to consider when conducting an assessment of high expectations in your school. Even if your school is not staffed by teachers of the same culture as the students, this list offers ways to build in high expectations for all students; ways to break down the cycle of tracking white students into gifted programs while poor and African American and Latino students are referred to special education classes in disproportionate numbers or are assumed to be aiming for vocational education.

CLASSROOM AND BUILDING ASSESSMENT: HIGH EXPECTATIONS

_____ Materials and examples used in class include works, ideas, and concepts by a diverse group of authors, thinkers, historical figures, and so on.

_____ Diverse groups are woven into, not separated out of, the overall curriculum.

_____ Texts, content, topics are chosen with the knowledge of what issues can arise with their introduction. Thought is given beforehand about how to provide a place for safe discussion.

_____ All students are made to feel safe in the classroom, hallways, lunchroom, everywhere in the school.

_____ Generalizations about racial and ethnic groups are simply not part of the vocabulary of the school.

_____ Evidence of many cultures can be seen on the walls, in the library, in the adults in the building, in examples used in classrooms, in literature, in celebrations, and so forth.

_____ Students' and parents' discomfort, frustration, anger are taken seriously and ways of mediation and discussion are provided to work things out.

_____ High expectations are provided for all students: to get work in, to complete work, to know the answers to different levels of questions, to work in class, to follow class guidelines, to respond to parent calls, to respond to structure.

_____ Parents of color are present and feel welcome at conferences, celebrations, dinners, and are part of parent councils, parent advisory groups.

_____ Students of all ethnicities are in all levels of learning in a building, that is, there are no "all white" or "all students of color" tracks or programs.

_____ Students of color are counseled to consider college, or other academic programs.

_____ Administration and teachers are willing to counter racist comments and low expectations of students of color in lounges, meetings, individual discussions, committee meetings.

_____ Teachers are aware of the importance of inclusive curriculum and education even when schools are primarily white: a matter of telling the complete truth.

_____ Teachers and staff are comfortable in discussing issues of race, class, and gender without being defensive or being shamed.

_____ Teachers and staff are willing to do the hard work of dealing with racism in the building and are willing to change when that is necessary.

_____ Teachers and staff are confident in their ability to talk about and deal with issues of race and inclusiveness, aware that these issues are always in flux and will learn new things each day that may make them uncomfortable.

_____ Teachers are willing to reach out intellectually, meet face to face, and step out and into another environment to work toward activism and enlightenment.

LESSON 35: LESSONS LEARNED

On Christmas Eve, 1968, I called my parents to tell them the name we had chosen for our son: Aaron David Landsman.

Silence.

Mother's voice came through, troubled.

"What? What have you decided on?"

"Aaron David."

"Oh. How did you decide on that, Sweetie?"

"The sound of it. We like the sound of it."

My father growled and got off the line. For the rest of his life he hesitated over the name Aaron David because of its Hebraic lilt, that very sound we love.

When I say the full name out loud, even now I hear the stillness of the desert or a mournful song. It is Jewish and Protestant and neither. Yet, to my father, "Aaron David" was never New England Wasp enough. Over the years he referred to Aaron as "AD" or "Big A." To me, AD sounded like the nickname of a man who owned a yacht and ate lobster on Nantucket Island. It did not sound ethnic or other; it sounded Protestant.

For a while I had no direction. Motherhood wasn't enough and I felt guilty because it wasn't. I loved my son deeply, yet never decorated our house each holiday like many women. I never cut out turkeys and put them on the windows or made homemade play dough.

Then, from 1970 to 1973 a group of women met every month to talk about what we wanted to do with our lives. A new wave of feminism was sweeping Carleton. For me, these meetings and the long talks over lunch in the one restaurant in town turned my future from gray to color. They gave me the belief that I could live a life independent from, yet inclusive of, my role as mother, as wife.

Some husbands planned trips to pornographic movies on the nights the meetings were held. Or they would drink beer at the apartment just below us, pushing on the ceiling with baseball bats, disrupting our talk with loud banging. Maury never participated in their evenings, but I barely appreciated his early feminist stance. He and I were fighting about absurd things, yelling about burnt toast or dirty diapers. I married a man who likes control, yet in a different context, in a more intimate struggle.

Finally, I found myself beginning to feel on equal ground with him. I began to refuse to be part of every endless dinner with his students, his colleagues. I decided to get my teaching credentials from Carleton. While Maury and I continued to fight, small things got done without tension, and we resumed dinners with couples we both liked. I began to see that the real battle was about my own struggle to define what I wanted to do. I began to fight Maury and not my father. Instead of a symbol of control, Maury became himself.

In those years, when we met in our women's group, talking about the fact that there were few women on the tenured or even untenured faculty, or women in administrative roles on campus, few black women were present in our lives. Mary Easter did not come to these meetings. I believe the criticism of this first wave of new feminism was right when it pointed out the lack of women of color in the mix. We were not aware of our whiteness as a racial component at all. I spent these years focusing not on race so much as on my place as a woman in history or work. I was free to ignore the role race played in my life. And how many times I do this now, I don't know.

I believe that the lack of true understanding of the role of race in the lives of women of color, by many in the feminist movement at the time, kept us from making important alliances with each other.

Patricia Ball Scott and Barbara Smith (2003) describe this in the book, *But Some of Us Are Brave: Women's Studies.* Black women who participated in the feminist movement during the 1960s often met with racism. It generally took the form of exclusion: black women were not invited to participate on conference panels which were not specifically about black or Third World women. They were not equally, or even proportionately, represented on the faculty of women's studies departments, nor were there classes devoted specifically to the study of black women's history. In most women's movement writings, the experiences of white, middle class women were described as universal "women's experiences," largely ignoring the differences of black and white women's experiences due to race and class.

Part of the overwhelming frustration black women felt within the women's movement was at white feminists' unwillingness to admit to their racism. This unwillingness comes from the sentiment that those who are oppressed cannot oppress others.

I see it now in our schools, in the tension between white women and black women in administration, in classroom instruction and faculty interaction. Because I believed that the situation of women was identical for both white and black women, because I did not read or hear the voices of black women at the time I was influenced by feminism, I did not explore these differences between us or the ways we were similar.

Students need to see modeled before them white and black women interacting openly and honestly with each other. Just as one of my bosses in a public school program insisted that Hamner, a charismatic black group leader, sit and read his college books while he was guarding the halls or on lunch duty so that students could get used to seeing a black man reading constantly, I believe we must model interaction between us, white and black, Native and white so that students see the possibilities of trust and collaboration constantly before them. I learned from black women's response to the so-called women's liberation movement at the time I was at Carleton that when we do not do this, when we do not see before us ways of arguing, disagreeing, coming together, we will not learn how to have the conversation, the interaction that will enlighten us all.

> *Reflection*: What groups are you in that give you a sense of power? Does your church, athletic team do this? In what context to do you feel in control, that you have real choices? Are these groups integrated? Do you tend to equate gender and race prejudice? As a woman, do you feel you have the same experiences as your black or white counterparts? If you are male, do you feel gender affects the way you live? In what ways?

> *Suggestions*: Figure out how to create a network of support groups for students of all kinds. Design your classes in ways to give students a chance to feel a sense of control of their education: contracts for grades, choice of literature or projects. Set up a faculty and staff women's support group with women of color included from the beginning. Begin the sometimes uncomfortable discussions about race together.

LESSON 36: THE ARTS AS A WAY IN

Our last year in Northfield, after Maury had decided to go to law school the following fall, I got a job teaching learning disabled students at the middle school there. I had been taking classes at Carleton toward a teaching certificate. The summer before my new job started, I went to the city to take special education classes at the University of Minnesota. Those days surrounded by the sounds and smells of Minneapolis in the summer, the kids on the basketball courts, the dialects and accents, I felt at home. I have traveled to many places since—Paris and Rome, Tuscany in the hills, Umbria in the mountains, Pokara, Nepal, at the base of the Anna Purna range, Stockholm, Oslo, Bangkok, and Hanoi—and I have felt the same ease of breath when I arrive at a city skyline with its geometric mixture of bridges and clotheslines, arches and edges. So I am sure that my unhappiness at Carleton, both then and later, had to do with its smallness, its architectural as well as cultural uniformity.

For that 1972–1973 school year in Northfield I had a tiny office/classroom in the middle school. This room was behind the auditorium, in back of the balcony, with a window up high and a wall that slanted down one side. Into this room came kids in trouble, kids who could not read or write, kids who were already beginning to skip school, those who slept out by the Cannon River to get away from their fathers when their fathers were drunk and took to hauling them out of bed at night and throwing them down stairs or onto the floor, kicking out at thin ribs and fragile elbows. One boy lived on a farm and began to drift to sleep by noon each day. He had been up at 4 a.m. to milk, or feed the pigs. He turned out to be a fine artist. As a reward for doing his work, and to keep him up, I let him have one wall in this hidden room. After he completed his assignment with me, he could paint a mural there. Some of my most peaceful afternoons, David would be painting and I would be doing paperwork and the sun would finally find our space.

It was the economic and social variety of students, from farm kids to faculty kids to combinations of the two, from poor kids to rich kids to kids whose parents worked at 3M Manufacturing that I loved then. The deer David drew began to leap out of the wall at me as I arrived in that back cubicle.

It was during this year, as the students with learning disabilities sang to me or drew for me or acted out their stories for me, that I became convinced that we can reach students in public schools most effectively through the arts: be it creative writing, dance, music, or painting. This belief in story, in voices, in expression as a way to feel in control has stayed with me until now, age sixty-four, as I sit and write my own story.

Over the last thirty-five years I have been a writer in the schools, a library "poet lady," and an English teacher in an alternative school. I have given talks and held dialogues, and my belief grows even stronger that the place to connect with students, the place to cross all sorts of lines and cultures, is in the telling of the tale, the singing of the song. It is in color and mural, in photo and dance, hip hop and blues. If we begin to worry about test preparation as a girl tells us of her anxiety about her new foster home or her love of staying up late, or as a boy worries aloud about his brother in Iraq, then we need to get out of this profession.

Many students now, at age eighteen, tell me that some of the most important things they learned in school were not the subjects taught, but were the relationships, the ethical discussions, the situations in school or in the city where they lived and the dialogue around those events that meant the most to them. One student remembered his teacher taking time to spend a week on immigration and culture when a new group of Hmong students from refugee camps in Thailand were about to enter his school. Because the week was spent on immigration in context, in the way it made our country what it is today, it felt natural and important in his life and the life of the community to talk about it at just that time. It was strategically placed to allow for positive anticipation of Hmong families who were soon to arrive.

Another teacher in the same school asked elders of the communities surrounding her building to come and talk with students about their own lives and histories. Many of these were artists: Somali poets, Latino novelists, or African American pianists. Through the arts and through the examples of artists that looked like those who lived around him, one student said he learned to express much of what was worrying him, and to escape these worries for a while, throwing pots, drawing, or playing drums.

As the demand grows, as subjects are cut, as arts are seen as "fringe" classes or luxuries, it becomes a form of antiracist activism to advocate for their central role in education.

The last year in Northfield, 1972, as Haiphong Harbor was bombed and Nixon won reelection, there was eventually a ceasefire in Viet Nam. At this time also, *Our Bodies Ourselves* found women speaking out loud about rape. It was a spectacular year for me in its liberation. I got my teaching credential in English, began my work in graduate education toward certification in learning disabilities, and found my place in the work world. Aaron was growing into a smiling and strangely mellow toddler, and Maury and I had negotiated our roles, had come through the years with our marriage still in tact, women's movement and all.

Because my mother's family had money, because of the cultural and social capital I still had as a white woman from a well-off family, I had a small amount of money given to me by my parents around this time. We spent it on a down payment for our first house in Minneapolis, where we were moving. Thus the change was seamless in a privileged way.

Reflection: When did you learn to draw, paint, play music, perform in a play? How important were these activities for you? How important are they for your students?

Suggestions: Think of ways to combine courses into interdisciplinary combinations: music and math, home economics and chemistry, literature and social studies, shop and sociology. Think of combinations you would not ordinarily put together and imagine how it might be done.

8

There Are No Short Cuts

LESSON 37: WORKING CONDITIONS

A gray winter day, Mavis Staples, gospel singer, and her husky voice moves words along. I sit years later waiting to see what emerges when I observe this city self. The small white town is left behind.

For the first three years I lived one block from the Mississippi River, which spirals through the cities of Minneapolis and St. Paul, I taught in suburbs. The first year I taught in Forest Lake, an hour away, and two years in Mounds View, twenty minutes on a good drive day. I was gradually getting closer and closer to the city where there were no jobs but where I wanted to teach. Maury began law school, and I was the breadwinner. My life in these first schools was again one of whiteness.

It was also one of class privilege. Nancy, a home economics teacher, said, trying to sign me up for one of the two competing teacher unions: "You don't want to join that federation, Julie. It is the same one that represents carpenters and plumbers. You are a professional."

I remember responding to her by saying something about my brother who lived on a commune and worked with his hands, and something about Uncle Otts, Maury's uncle who was a printer in Baltimore and came home ink-stained and tired at four in the morning, and how his family tiptoed through their lives for years so he could sleep as the sun shone. I told her I would be proud to be in any organization that included them. (I am sure I was unbearable in my self-righteousness.)

My first year as the special educator, I took many students whom teachers simply disliked. More than one of these teachers physically threw students into my room some days, pushing them toward my desk, yelling at them the whole time. The schools were devoted to whiteness without stating or even being aware of this. I was not aware of it myself, busy with David and Dana, Susan and John, who began to wait at my door, kicked out of English for the sixth day in a row, out of shop because they came late and challenged the teacher.

In my second and third years, in a suburb closer to home, I became aware that some teachers did not want to work with the Bailey twins or with any of the kids from the trailer court in the middle of a district of wealthy homes. Others included them and reached them in ways that were amazing. There was one black family in the entire middle school; the Brewster kids were going through the system quiet and obedient. I noticed this, yet by then I was trying to create a place of welcome for rejected white boys who had learning disabilities, or who were jittery with hyperactivity.

There are years when you are so busy, raising your child, taking over as your husband goes off to school each night, barely grabbing a five o'clock dinner together, that you twirl in a dizzy spin of juggling, and you do not stop to gain perspective, understand history, housing patterns, or the context in which you live. It is hard to describe the busyness of a regular teaching day, to capture how crazy life can feel once September comes: the jigsaw of interaction in the five minutes between classes or the twenty-two minutes over lunch, the feat that teachers must pull off.

If we could change the working conditions of teachers, giving them fewer students per hour, giving them decent preparation time and a full half hour for lunch at least (not counting the five minutes to shut up their classroom and the five minutes to open it up again), we would get further in the struggle for reconstructing education for equity and justice. If we could provide more teachers with meaningful time off, not just for one four-hour workshop, but for a month or two of intensive study, bringing the results of this back to their districts, we might make progress in so many areas ten times faster than we are now, including multicultural education. Because of low salaries, many teachers work in the summer

Staff development days are often spent learning new forms to fill out, listening to speeches by many who have not been in a school district on a daily basis for years. And all the while teachers in those required sessions are worried about the over two hundred students who will arrive in their classrooms the next day. To make training meaningful means to change radically the working conditions under which teachers teach.

Working conditions are part of the struggle for educational equity and inclusive classrooms. This does not excuse racist language or even curriculum, nor does it mean we cannot provide real multicultural education for students now. It does mean that the fight for time to prepare, to study, to meet with parents, to go out to neighborhoods, to schedule field trips, is part of the fight for social justice in our schools.

Many teachers in high schools in Minneapolis who are facing classes of forty-five students each hour are telling me they know what they need to do but they can't do it. Logistically it is not possible to meet the individual needs of over two hundred students. And it is devastating to go to work each day knowing you cannot do what needs be done.

Reflection: What is your teaching day like? How much time do you have to read during the day? How much time to meet with other teachers? How much time do you have to plan for the next day, or to grade papers?

Suggestions: Find ways to read or draw or daydream. Skip the lounge. Turn off the lights in your classroom during lunch. Talk with others about how to achieve some time to work. Stay one hour later if you can in order to bring less work home on as many days as possible.

LESSON 38: THE FRONT OFFICE

It was not until my third year, living on 46th Avenue in Minneapolis, Aaron settled into school in the city, that I began to explore issues of race and equity in any depth. When it came time to send Aaron off to public school, we looked carefully. Maury went to parent days, sat on tiny chairs in elementary classrooms, and felt the condescension when administrators or teachers said, in syrupy voices, "and isn't it great to have some *daddies* here! My goodness!"

The school we chose was Pratt Elementary. After getting a sense of each of the different programs, we liked its Continuous Progress model where students were with the same teachers for two years. This school was also just across the river from our home. Maury liked the straightforward talk of the principal, the integrated classrooms, the old wooden doorways and polished oak floors. He liked its "cityness," its location off University Avenue, not far from where he had a part-time job with the state public defender. It was a school in demand, popular for its good teachers and principal.

We ultimately got Aaron in because of his whiteness. There were a high percentage of African American students in this building, and Aaron would help balance the numbers. So, while it meant a slightly longer bus ride, it was the one that we chose; especially after our neighbors took their newly adopted Korean child to the school even closer and the secretaries asked them to keep him off their countertop in the office because he "probably had diseases."

It is in these initial contacts with children, in the first time a parent sets foot in the door, that impressions are formed and cooperation is possible. I have been at schools where parents are made to feel welcome, are treated with respect by secretaries, clerks, and building engineers. I have also been in high schools where parents are treated with suspicion, or ignored completely when they enter the main office. In these latter buildings it was often parents of color who were given the cold shoulder. This makes all the difference in how community members feel about even entering the doors of their son's or daughter's school.

The most perceptive superintendents and administrators insist that the entire building be part of diversity work, any dialogues around issues of race and culture. This includes building engineers, hall monitors, clerks and secretaries, as well as educational assistants. Even better, they look to hire those in their front offices, in their engineer rooms, in their hallways, from the community of the kids themselves. They are also those principals who are constantly looking for good teachers and staff of color as well.

Perhaps an analogy can be made to the role of the nurse versus the doctor. The nurse does as much, or often more, nurturing, keeping track, day-to-day observation of those in her or his care than do doctors. We get our feeling about the medical building, the doctor's office, often from the way we interact with nurses. There are buildings where hall and security guards, nurses and secretaries can tell you much more about what is going on with a child, or in the neighboring community, than the teacher in the classroom down the hall.

Not only would including these workers in the training be advantageous for them, it would also benefit the teachers and principals, counselors and social workers in the building to have their input. It is one way we might also begin to have discussions about race, as many educational assistants and secretaries are people of color while teachers are white.

My son walked by himself down the halls of Pratt on his first day of school. He asked to go alone to his classroom. He turned to wave as he opened the door on the first floor where he would spend two of his six years in this school. The year was 1974 and Nixon would resign, Boston would face white mobs as it began to integrate the schools there and the Viet Nam war would end with mass evacuations and deaths as desperate people scrambled for helicopters. I experienced all this from newspapers, and even felt some of the effects as Vietnamese refugees began to settle in our city.

Minneapolis is one of the most segregated cities in the nation, by race and poverty even now. It was a bastion of anti-Semitism during the 1930s and 1940s. In 1949, at the same time the Minneapolis American Automobile Association would not accept Jewish members, the president of the AAA in St. Paul, just across the river, was a Jew. This is how different the two cities were and still can be.

For these years, as Aaron went off on his orange bus in the dark winter mornings and I drove out to suburban schools, we were settling in, walking the river each evening together when we could, making new friends, enjoying the bridges and arches that frame our lives even now.

Reflection: How are people welcomed into your building? How are they viewed?

Suggestions: Consult those who work as attendance clerks, hall monitors, secretaries about a child you are concerned about. Help set up discussions and training sessions for all staff and teachers. Make this part of the negotiations for different unions in your district.

LESSON 39: GETTING COMFORTABLE

In 1976, I got a job in the city at a public school called the YES Center. This was a program for middle school students who were kicked out of their home schools for disruptive behavior. It is here I learned about race in a new context and about the street life of many students both white and black. It was here that I saw institutional racism at its most blatant. Schools clamored to send us their black and Native youth, while white students with serious problems remained in their buildings tearing up the halls or even the classrooms

While I had a lot to learn in this special education site, I also felt more at home in this city school than I had felt since my library center job ten years before. I was working with students who were bright and restless and in trouble. And this school resonated with my work in DC the summers when I was meeting with people in their apartments and houses, getting to understand the neighborhoods. It also echoed New Haven. I could see Idell, Darnell, or Rodell from my library job here: older, skipping out at lunchtime, or running around the cafeteria with someone's food. I could see Melvin in the boys I worked with, eager to capture on paper the dialogue, the words they knew. Somehow this place felt as though it was part of a logical progression of places, while my time in Northfield and the suburbs felt like a break, even a disruption in that progression.

I want to say here, that this feeling is not meant to discount or put down those teachers who work in the suburbs or rural settings. I believe there is a place for teachers who want to change attitudes, who want to make sure both rich and poor kids are heard, who want to create vibrant classrooms, in *any* school, in *any* location. I know friends who love the green and spacious feel of their suburban yards, or others who love farmland and open country. There is just as much to do out there, if not more, in the area of multicultural curriculum, support for students of color, for staff training, as there is in the city. Many teachers feel they must work in a thoroughly multicultural and diverse school to make a difference. I have seen brilliant white teachers in wealthy suburbs teach culturally rich courses, open the eyes of students and colleagues to issues of social justice, and make a huge impact where they are. This work is an equal opportunity challenge.

The lesson I take from my own moves and resettling is that it is best to respond to where we want to be with our emotions, with our desires, and to try and teach there. It is not to glamorize those who work in cities.

The first months at the YES Center I was naive and talked to kids in ways that called on my middle class, white vocabulary. I believe I spoke with condescension, treating my streetwise students like children.

"Oh, Johnny, where are you from? That's nice. A nice neighborhood I am sure."

"Jamal, I am sure you can get here on time if you just try harder."

"I hope your mom can make it to talk with me tomorrow."

I was not being truthful. I knew Johnny's neighborhood was tough. I did not try and find out why Jamal was not getting to school on time, which ultimately had to do with a sister he was watching until his mother got home from her night shift.

To think that any parent, much less a parent who could lose a day's pay and perhaps even his or her job, could come to see me at the last minute was extremely unrealistic. These comments and others were greeted with slumped shoulders, sarcastic smiles, and outright anger.

I also created simple-looking worksheets for my students who had learning disabilities. These resembled elementary school plans, with primary type and babyish references or transparently easy sentences. Because these students could not read well I brought in children's books.

They caught on to me early and did not like it. Jamal told me to find some "real work for a man to do." Johnny suggested I go teach where there were smaller kids. I knew within the first week that I was in trouble. And yet all this time students kept coming back. And we did laugh. And we did work together.

There were as many black staff as there were white and they, as well as the students, ultimately guided me. I found books that looked like regular teenage novels, written at a second or third grade level for the students who were reading at that level. I made up exercises and lessons that called on concepts from the neighborhoods, politics, culture, regardless of reading level. These were students who may have had problems reading but who at the same time were strategic thinkers.

The diversity of staff and teachers was deliberate, providing a constant model of interaction between blacks and whites so that students would witness collaboration every day. It became logical to them to see black, white, and Native, men and women, working together.

In this new place I experienced my whiteness more powerfully than I had ever experienced it before—not because of an article on privilege or research or extensive training, but rather because it was an obvious part of my identity there. Race was an ongoing part of our conversations, our meetings, our struggle to find solutions. Thus, years later, when I finally read articles on privilege, when whiteness became a topic of conferences and research, I felt as though someone had given a name to, and concrete description of, what I had lived with for years. And while I was not as savvy about it as I would be after I read Peggy McIntosh, or James Banks, I had been made aware of being white, of having money, of having an entrée into the white world, both in DC and now in Minneapolis, long before the conceptual knowledge I gained from articles and books. I was experiencing Professor Joe White's dialogue and for a while was in his "place of discomfort."

In this building, with its hall guards and its student group sessions at the end of the day or our faculty "war councils" in the middle of a tough morning, I was not successful at first. Yet soon something clicked. It fell into place: I resonated with the kids and with their stories. I felt more relaxed with the staff, with their laughter and tough love and in the feeling of commitment toward finding a way for students to succeed in school.

I worked with black men—Bob Johnson, assistant principal; Hamner Williams, hall monitor and group leader; Harry Grigsby, building engineer and group leader—to learn how to reach the young men and women in my reading classes. Also there were black women, Mae Gossett and Arlene Sanders, who helped me understand my strength as a teacher of kids in trouble. These individuals and white men and women like Jeff Burk, Mary Kay Carlson, and the principal, Tom Kitto, who had been teaching in the cities for years, were all part of my transformation from uncertain and anxious teacher to a teacher with confidence. They knew how to warn me when a lesson would not connect, and also how to compliment me after my students finally learned measurement or became fluent in decoding multisyllable words.

Gradually students talked with me in adult conversations. We discussed ethical dilemmas they were facing out on the streets, peer pressure to shoplift or skip school, the drug dealing that was going on in the apartment nearby. When I stopped, in January, to look at where we had come together, I realized I had learned as much from them as they had from me. I began to know their neighborhoods intimately after leaving them off at home or going out to round them up to bring them into school in the YES Center van.

I also developed confidence. I did not pretend to be black or even hip. I learned over time that students did not want a new friend. The wanted someone in control who was compassionate, who would demand the kind of behavior and skills they would need to return to their "home schools." All of them knew they were with us because they were in trouble.

During these first years in city schools I lived surrounded by black dialect in its everyday expression, kids teaching me new words all the time. I learned how to build on students' strengths to translate this black English into a form of speaking and writing that they would need as they went through the white-oriented, formal English world. We even taught all our students, white and black, to say "Cognitive Restructuring Center" for our timeout area so that when they gave tours of our program to school board members they would impress them with their multisyllable terminology. I also learned that what sounds "black" to most people is actually spoken by many white kids who have spent much of their time on the streets.

I learned here that mere love of the kids was not enough. I had to learn about their lives, their neighborhoods, their way of negotiating the city to be able to teach them. During this time I met black women dressed in suits and high couture, and white parents in stained shirts and old pants and white men in pin stripes and black men in jeans and t-shirts on parent nights. I learned gradually not to form preconceived notions about anyone. Even now I relearn this. I learned in new ways about a buffer of class and race that had protected me from tough times, and that I had had that buffer most of my life.

In this context I was never made to feel guilty or shamed for what I did not know about culture or poverty. I was just expected to catch on quickly. I changed how I spoke and the kids responded.

This clear and kind expectation and instruction has been true all my life, from the first lesson Jean taught me in that Dallas kitchen to the meeting a few days ago to train for an oral history project on the north side of Minneapolis.

The consistency of faith in me to learn, faith in me to treat each student with justice and a firm hand, faith in me to take each new concept and absorb it, rather than fight it, faith in me to keep my own radar and self-respect in tact, is what has led me with relative smoothness along these city streets, these hallways filled with kids of such complexity and beauty.

In the next few years our program was relocated to a new and different part of town. In this almost all African American neighborhood we worked during summers in addition to the regular school year with kids in trouble with the courts or the school system or both. I began to keep a journal, returning again and again to writing as my way of making sense of the world and the kids who stumbled into my room. I met kids who did not know what a salad was, and kids who read Jane Austen for fun but skipped school for whole years at a time. The mixture of young people in our program defied definition.

And all this time, I was learning how to teach students who could not read at age fourteen or who came and went from Indian reservations or who showed up angry from day one. When a young man exploded in my room after I asked about his mother, Bob Johnson, the assistant principal, filled me in about this young man and his mother's situation, with facts, with suggestions, never implying I should have known, that I should have acted in any other way than I did. No one came to train us about how to learn about culture or class or what students needed. We simply were doing it as we went along. And because it was part of our struggle together as a team, in a small program, with many meetings and interactions at lunch or breaks, we absorbed change in student populations, culture, class, and neighborhood affiliation over time.

Each day something new could be added to the mix, to the tension or anger or sorrow. A parent could die, a brother could be shot, a pimp could enter the building looking for one of our female students. Those who wanted to work at the YES Center were self-selected. After a year, any teacher who did not feel they could work this way or felt it was not a match with his or her skills could leave. Thus we were a tight-knit collection of teachers, aides, secretaries, hall guards, group leaders, and administrators. I found all the expertise I needed right in this group. We appreciated new ideas, research, and suggestions. We wanted knowledge of the families and communities around us.

Yet we did not respond well to so-called experts. I am trying to describe something elusive here, having to do with the difference between conceptual knowledge and experiential knowledge. It has to do with being kind to ourselves as we blunder and kind to new and experienced teachers who venture into this territory for the first time. At the YES Center, race, because it was understood as being on the table, did not intrude, or even startle. It simply was.

It is so clear now that gaining experience, learning from veteran teachers all around me, was how I became good at what I did. To place inexperienced teachers in schools with the toughest students, or in schools with high rates of poverty, as they are often placed, is doing a serious disservice to those students and to the communities from which they come. Unless there is a critical mass of experienced teachers in these buildings to mentor new teachers as I was mentored, the school will often struggle needlessly. I still use what I learned on the job when I talk with students. I still call on instincts I developed over years in the classroom.

When many of the poorest students get even the most well-meaning new teachers with no understanding of the day to day, month to month, rhythm of teaching, they are being shortchanged. And because so many poor students are often students of color this compounds the disadvantages that have their roots in a racist history, perpetuating inequity every year and every day.

Reflection: Where are you the most comfortable, city or suburb or rural area? How important is this in your teaching location? What was your first year of teaching like? Your fifth? What did you learn in those years and afterwards?

Suggestions: Watch for new teachers in your building. Ask them out for coffee once in a while. Create a small community of like-minded teachers in your building and meet as often as you can. Include new teachers in this group.

LESSON 40: OVERREFERRAL TO SPECIAL EDUCATION

It was in my second year at the YES Center that I noticed the continual overreferral of kids of color to our site. Our program was filling up with black kids. I continually heard from other teachers about white kids who were intimidating teachers, threatening secretaries, or skipping school three out of five days a week. Yet these students were often kept in their home buildings despite outrageous behavior. One white fourteen-year-old boy spray-painted a room where teachers and the principal were meeting in his regular school. It was not until then that they referred him to our program. He had been throwing chairs, tearing up books, running the halls for a year before the episode with the paint.

We had a thin, young white boy who walked out on third floor ledges if we did not keep an eye on him. If he did manage to get out, he threatened to jump. It took four grown men to wrestle his wild, turning, churning body into quiet. By comparison to these extremely disturbed white students, many of the black students in our school were actually quite rational and more easily reached through group sessions and small classes.

That these very disturbed white kids were often left too long without the help of an alternative setting, while we filled our seats with black students who were simply interested in the streets and the action there, and who were not "disturbed," is an illustration of how skewed our perception can be when we consider disability or emotional disturbance.

This situation is as present today, years after it was recognized as a problem, as it was in 1973 when I taught at the YES Center. Black males are referred to special education programs in much higher numbers than their percentage of the school population. In an article published in 1999, Kimberly Peterz described this situation concisely:

The overrepresentation of Black students, especially Black males, is due to biased testing and the cultural misunderstanding of Black people. Some educators responsible for teaching Black students are not aware of the cultural differences and backgrounds of Black students, and therefore view these differences as learning disability (Reschly, 1980). Researchers who question the practices that lead to this disproportionate and overrepresentation of Black students in particular types of special education classrooms suggest that this phenomena may occur in part because of biased testing practices (Reschly, 1980), and because of the cultural differences of Black students and the way the educators view these differences (Gilbert & Gay, 1985). (Peterz, 1999)

Because the diagnosis for categories of emotional disturbance and behavior problems in special education is so subjective, based on teacher observation and narrative, this is the category where we find the most overreferral. It taps our deepest subconscious racism to assume disturbance or lack of intelligence in the behavior of black males. The bias of IQ testing itself has been thoroughly documented and thus accounts for other categories of overreferral: learning disability or mental retardation. Concrete physical categories such as orthopedically handicapped or hearing impaired do not see such overreferral.

Years after I left the YES Center, primarily white boys would shoot up whole groups of students in their high schools. Yet I did not hear many people commenting on violence in the "white community" as these stories of shootings continued. As we have seen so tragically on the Red Lake Indian Reservation and at Virginia Tech, Native and Asian students can encompass among their midst disturbed and violent young men, too. Some insightful studies and books are being written about the gender of these shooters, about what is driving young men of all kinds to such violence.

I still see Glenn, the young white boy we took into our program in mid-January who went out on ledges. He is perched there looking down three floors over a highway, outside his math teacher's room. His eyes are blank, his body tense, fearful, and yet determined. Around him, inside the room, are his after-school group, primarily black males. They are talking to him gently, softly, knowing that any yelling, any excitement will set him off. Finally they talk him into climbing down and coming into the room where the group leader, two cops, and the principal are waiting for him.

For years Glenn was not referred to us. It was only after we demanded white students to match the numbers of black students that he arrived. Racism in special education and referral does not only harm the kids wrongly referred, it harms those who need help and who are not given it.

At the end of my second year at the YES Center, Maury and I and Aaron moved from our house on 46th Avenue to a larger one on 43rd Avenue. On the cold November day we made the shift, a team of people from my school came to help out, loading the truck on one block and unloading it three blocks away. The new block was similar to the old one, in that it was primarily white and working and middle class, bordering on the wealthy River Road houses. Aaron could stay in his integrated elementary school.

By this time Tom Kitto, the head of the YES Center, had been able to stipulate to the committee in special education that made placements into our program, that we must get white referrals in the same numbers as kids of color.

Reflection: Who do you refer to special education? What group makes up the majority of special education students in your school? What categories are they referred in? Why do you think this is true?

Suggestions: Review the sidebar. Consider changing the situation of overreferral. How can your school address this, given these factors?

FINDING SOLUTIONS TO OVERREFERRAL

Determine the questions to consider.

Study culturally relevant pedagogy.

Evaluate early childhood education.

Reevaluate assessment tools and process—criterion referenced not standardized.

Improve communication with parents.

Encourage extended family involvement.

Provide cross-cultural competence training and support for teachers.

Insist on school district oversight of motives for referrals.

Design behavior-oriented programs—allow for choice and self-determination.

Provide mentoring: for students and for teachers.

Avoid one-size-fits-all approach.

Work for true collaboration between regular and special education.

Offer extensive resources for teachers and staff: training, community liaisons, parent organizations that are culturally sensitive and effective, and so on.

Be willing to have open and honest explorations into the unconscious bias in our own upbringing, media influence, family instruction. Provide real training in understanding privilege (racial, economic, gender) and how this plays out in our schools without us even intending it to or knowing we are part of it.

Honestly explore the practice of tracking: from giftedness to special education, advanced classes to vocational instruction.

9

Moments of Vision, Moments of Dissonance

LESSON 41: GOING TO PLACES OF DISCOMFORT

Images fragment around me as I try and describe these twenty-five years, the center of my life, burning on all burners, family, writing, and schools. Chronology and incidents coalesce around race: meetings and funerals, arguments and collaboration. And accompanying this, interwoven into every part of it, were my fumbling and awkward attempts to understand the Wasp thoughts and impulses that lingered in me.

There is a phenomenon often attributed to aging. We can capture in clear detail images from years and years ago much more accurately than we can capture yesterday. I find this part of the book, about my last twenty years, the toughest to write. So I include here a series of scenes that stand out to me, that reveal something about my white life in a diverse world. I have documented my thoughts on race in schools in *Basic Needs: A Year with Street Kids in a City School*, in *A White Teacher Talks about Race,* and in *White Teachers/Diverse Classrooms* coedited with Chance Lewis. I do not want to repeat the content of those books.

About eight years ago, many years after we moved into our new house, an African Canadian woman, coming to look at houses before she moved to Minneapolis, gave me a call. Uju was bringing her family with her from Edmonton and after three days of driving around with a real estate broker, she wondered why he was showing her only places on the north side of the city in the primarily black section of Minneapolis. She would be working at the university on the south side, near where we lived. She had made it clear she wanted to be within walking distance of the university campus, if possible.

In the year 2000 Uju was being *steered*. Because of her skin color, she was being limited to a choice of homes far from her place of work. Because of her vulnerability as a visitor from out of town, the realtor thought he could get away with this.

After Uju told the realtor that she thought he was steering her, he did show her a few more places nearer the campus. But by the end of her week here she had almost given up, deciding to forgo the move altogether. I had mentioned a house across from us for sale by owner. On good days she could walk to work. She came to our home, met with the women selling the house, and signed the agreement that night, moving in a few months later.

I remember sitting with her after the phone calls were made, banks contacted, and her husband, Tolowa, consulted. I remember the silence for a moment. I was so aware of it all, the three wasted days, the coldness that was part of her first impressions, and I don't mean the temperature outside. As it turned out, the university library system did not use her to her full potential and Yale lured her away two years after she arrived.

What all this makes clear, as when black friends are stopped for no reason walking to church in a "good" neighborhood, when Latino friends' children are automatically placed in lower track classrooms, when brown skinned kids are followed in stores, while their white friends are left alone, was this: my black friends continue to experience this country differently. Oh, we build bridges, work on community projects together, teach together, have dinner and drink wine together. Yet still, in many contexts we are teaching, living different lives.

I recently read an article about something called "micro aggressions." These are the small slights that people of color, often middle and upper class, experience during their work life. The accumulation of these slights makes certain days, months, even years, frustrating. Some people of color interviewed for the article said they did not feel these were of consequence to them, others said they built up into depression or anger. I find myself recognizing, again, that I don't have to deal with this at all, either to build a thick skin or respond when these slights happen.

Students sometime simply want to reason such things through. By making classrooms a place where puzzling it out can happen, where judgment is suspended while we go through a student's confusion, we are creating a space for safe dialogue. This suspension does not mean we agree with the student, it simply means we will puzzle it out with him or her, given what we know.

Virginia Woolf (1953) describes in *A Writer's Diary* something about marriage that I have experienced at various times in my life around the subject of race.

> Arnold Bennett says that the horror of marriage lies in its "dailiness." All acuteness of relationship is rubbed away by this. The truth is more like this: life—say 4 days out of 7—becomes automatic; but on the 5th day a bead of sensation (between husband and wife) forms which is all the fuller and more sensitive because of the automatic customary unconscious days on either side. That is to say the year is marked by moments of great intensity. Hardy's "moments of vision." How can a relationship endure for any length of time except under these conditions? (p. 96)

Precisely because of the "dailiness of interaction," those moments of vision can happen. And such revelations come as gifts, even if they are accompanied by pain or even shame, and anger. They come when someone points out that we have referred to the blackness of some individuals while never referring to the whiteness of others. They come when we are amazed at the complexity of understanding of Jane Austen by our student with a baby, who is struggling to get to school, and someone points out that there is no reason she, too, cannot comprehend what we are trying to teach. They come when we walk through certain halls filled with white students in an integrated school without noticing that this is where all the gifted, AP classes are, while downstairs in comprehensive classes the halls are filled with brown and black students. They come with the tears of a young man in our creative writing class, who stays late and talks of how tired he is when his white classmates refuse to believe his descriptions of being pulled from the postal jeep he is assigned, delivering mail in a white suburb, because the cops cannot conceive of a black postman in their territory.

The "dailiness of interaction": taking of attendance, walking to the lunchroom, teacher meeting arguments, and the rush for the copy machine; all these form the context around which Woolf's "moments of vision" can happen.

I witnessed one of these moments in an auditorium of five hundred teachers. I had given a keynote to teachers and staff in a district outside Minneapolis on one of those staff development days in August before school officially began for students. There was time for questions and answers. A brave white teacher stood up, turned to her district colleagues in a mixed suburb and told them that it was time "we all dealt with our own racism before we will change anything, any scores, any expectations, any behavior." Then she sat down. I realized, from the frozen silence that followed, that she had put herself out there and would live with the reaction of her colleagues, both hostile and supportive, long after I had left this session. And this reminded me again of those we left behind in Montgomery after the march with King.

Such moments can happen when a black man hesitantly says, in the quiet of your classroom at the end of teacher conferences, he believes, in his heart, "no offense to you," that white people mostly don't believe that black children hold the same value as human beings as white children. And all you can do is tell him you hope this is not true, that if it is, you hope this changes in your lifetime.

They come when there is no defensiveness in you. And you know that this man, that woman, senses this about you or they would not feel they could say these things in front of you.

Over the years I lived in the house on the corner of our block, I watched Rodney King's batterers get acquitted and understood the violence afterwards. Not condoned it, but understood the rage. I watched blacks and Latinos come to the rescue of whites in trouble on those streets in Los Angeles and never saw this emphasized in the mainstream news. I watched Ronald Reagan go to Bitburg Cemetery and offend us all as he stood where Nazi SS were buried, the same SS who organized and helped carry out the gassing of Jews. I worked for the passage of the Equal Rights Amendment for women and saw it defeated, unable to get the necessary states to ratify it. I have seen men go off to wars I do not believe in, and die, time after time.

During these years I have often felt helpless in the face of traditional media coverage that recycles stereotyped and incomplete views of so many groups of people. I have often felt discouraged by the cowardice in my own government, in assenting to policies that condemn not only my country but also other countries to destruction and chaos. And when this happens, when my despair kicks in, I do believe the classrooms, the poets, the work of the neighborhood brings some sanity to my worldview.

In the face of history, I have come back to morning in the classroom, the flower on the desk from the Hmong student who loves roses, the white kid with the freckles who has discovered limericks. I don't know how else we get through these days. Trying to achieve balance while knowing so much of the world, working in rooms across from McDonald's, in hallways near the railroad tracks, is how we stay human.

Reflection: Name some "moments of vision" in your life. What did they mean for you at the time? How did you change as a result of learning what you did? How do you remain hopeful during times of despair?

Suggestions: Take a "mental health" day. Do something you love unconnected to school. Go to a movie, draw, take a yoga class in the middle of the day.

LESSON 42: BECOMING OUTSIDER

In my home a block from the Mississippi River, I made some changes, some shifts in perception. Yet when I ventured out to other places, where a language that was not my own was spoken, I also absorbed an otherness, an outsider status, that has brought shifts in my way of understanding. This is knowledge that comes from going to a place of dissonance, a place where we are in the minority, whether it is in the southern United States for a northerner, or a country in Asia, up in the mountains, for a person from the United States.

In 2000, just two years before I would move from my home on 43rd Avenue to my present downtown space, Mary Easter asked if I would like to come with her and some friends to Nepal. Maury tagged along. When I came to the color, landscape, architecture, religion, language, and music in this place of both extreme beauty and extreme poverty, I felt disoriented. This chapter contains entries from my journal written in Nepal. I include them to try and capture the experience, to describe Professor White and Cones's place of dissonance in detail.

Pokhara, Nepal

Arrival

I am left alone while others walk. I sit and stare straight ahead at violet hills. Men run around serving tea and hoisting red sails. Men bring food, women bend in scarlet dhotis and lift children or water or sand. In deep blue gowns, draped with yellow shawls they raise brown arms above their heads, pound rocks and build temples. Here, men work too, stripped to the waist, white linen draped around their heads. They also hoist brick towards the window ledge to begin outlining the light that will enter the temple when people will lay supine on the ground, four, six times a day, as the young men do outside of Roosevelt High School, Minneapolis. Further beyond the town, figures move to carve the hillsides into curves of green for wheat.

What privilege this long white woman in tee shirt and skirt, drinking tea on the terrace, feels, to be alive at this moment.

Sun melts below deep purple hills as black birds carve pale evening into wings and deep shadow.

First Days

A woman draped in red stands along the side of the road. She asks for a cigarette. She talks with us, stays beside us, explains the words, "husband," "wife." She asks for money. She wants to know if we have a baby. She teaches us the word for baby. She wants a pen. Her eyes are warm. Yet, she makes me nervous.

We keep walking and I can feel when the woman in red melts away, her brown skin gone, her smile over.

Do you have money?

Yes, so much of it I wash myself over and over in hot, hot water.

Yes, I have money. So much money my house can get too warm even in winter and I always have water, clean water. So much money I can shop at a supermarket and buy extra oranges and let one grow rotten in the bottom of an uneven pottery bowl.

I have money, so much so that I am able to come here and walk by you on the curving road near Lake Fewa, through the rice fields and the terraced hills, by the small fires burning while children dance to the morning heat in wool caps and purple shirts, and I am allowed to smile at you and shake my head when you ask for money. I have so much money I am allowed to deny it to you, or to give it to you, who taught me the word for baby. I can keep on going to my hotel near the yellow boat and write about the way the air changed and light dimmed as you asked again and again, do you have? Do you have?

I have and have and have: music and a carpet and someone who waters my plants while I am gone.

And I have shoes and wool sweaters and new shawls made of the softest Pashmina and I have and have and have and you disappear. I keep walking, relieved you are gone, that I do not look behind me and see your red shawl, your warm eyes, your coffee skin, your jewels and do not hear the water bottle clanking against your thigh as you walk.

I do not have the words to describe you who teaches me Nepali, or the child along the way who clings to his mother, circled by dogs. I do not have the words, except to say, you disappeared and I did not see you go, did not have the chance to say good-bye, or good morning, *namasté*, to salute the god in you.

Washing Woman

A young woman washes her hair in the cold lake water. It is still before the burn off of mist, and Mozart is playing across the Nepali morning. She has on a scarlet belt and a gold skirt, and her hair is buried deep under the surface. It is cold and she is in the sun but there is her breath, later, in a cloud out from her mouth, as she lifts her face, and pulls up her green blouse and softens into the warmth of cloth. She cups water in her hands, washes her face and throws back her hair, as the suns reaches her where she squat-sits on stone. It takes time, cleaning, bending in frozen December in Nepal. The work of living takes time.

This is what we see all around us, and such delight in the leaning back, the child being groomed, sheer pleasure of being touched.

My mother gave me a red velvet dress when I was thirteen, and I had nothing to wear to a dance. She had been saving it for Christmas, but pulled it out of its tissue paper early; handed it to me. So little touch to this gift, but oh how I loved its softness next to my skin.

Here a young woman enters water. She will not dance in overheated rooms with pale boys who do not yet like music, do not like holding a girl in their arms but come anyway, their mothers calling them in from football, or under the hoods of their brothers' cars, to go to the final dance class of the autumn. Here, in Nepal, she will finish her work at the lake, while a girl in red velvet in Connecticut will go to a holiday dance and long for what she cannot name, the touch of someone, anyone, grooming her with touch, combing her hair.

"What do you plan to do with your wild and precious life?" says Mary Oliver in a poem that I keep in my notebook. I watch the boats unfurl themselves on the lake. I decide to answer her question:

Climb to the top of some important mountain in Nepal, the one with a name that starts with an S. Stand and decide that crystal is a color, that blue is a texture, that the small dark eyed child near the path the day before is shadow, and substance.

Back home, deliver meals to Helen's house again on Christmas or even a random Tuesday evening in April. Only Helen is not home and her long limbed nephew with bare feet answers the door, stepping over the black dog who barely turns at my arrival. Stand and breathe this man, woman's last air, last days, somewhere R&B on a radio, and somewhere back among the dirty dishes a cat raises its voice in protest or hunger.

Leave Helen's house, knowing protest and hunger are the same thing.

Stay at home in my book-lined room and write about the red of Nepal: figure out what connects the water buffalo who sleeps while birds dance on his back to the dog, off leash, who roams by the boathouse on the banks of the Mississippi just near the cave where the homeless men sleep, their whole universe on their backs in the morning near the river, mist coming in the way it does in Nepal.

Only Connect

Some girls here wake to a baby's cry in the morning, gather them up in blue cloth and hoist them onto backs too small for such a burden. They take them to the rice fields, and bend and straighten. The infants move with the curve of small spines, up and down in warming air until they drift to sleep, become heavier as the sun beats hot. Insects gather around sweat like flies to fly paper and the girls wipe away moisture.

Back home Tanya brings her daughter, Serena, into the classroom, sits with her on her lap, works on beading Serena's hair before first hour and for some strange reason you notice the neon pink of the sign for used cars across Bryant Avenue is the same color as the neon beads that warm the child's head, same color as a piece of wool around an old man's cap who sits on his front step in Nepal watching his daughter and baby in the rice field.

Circling Home

The early mornings are good; "*Namasté*" said through dark doorways as I go on my walk. In the afternoon a black cow delivers her calf in the center of stubble where a wedding goes on behind a pale yellow wall. All of it outside, the birthing, the marrying, and the morning meal where seven people in seven bright colors sit around a table and drink tea.

The days are like and like and like, the rain or the not rain, the sun or the not sun, the dark or the leaving dark, emerging light. And death or not death, birth or not birth. Nothing seems the opposite of the other, but rather is attached like a shadow, always part of what it is not.

And I wonder if I have to come half way around the world to learn such continuity: an old woman who carries a haystack on her back, bent so that she is food, fuel, roof and then, later, woman.

The sun moves toward not sun. Yet not sun here is sun in Minnesota, shining on my geraniums in the winter window. How good to be concerned with not words, with phrases of sound, color, sky, how good to see the shadow attached to each thing, making it whole.

Dawn to Dusk

If you get to Mike's patio by a certain hour, by a certain moment, you can see the egrets fly white on gray water, in scattering fragments, catching first light of day. If you stay at Mike's for a while and eat a banana pancake at ten, you will feel the hot sun begin to ease along your forehead, shoulder or back and know you have another day of yellow boat, square and loyal on the water below you as you taste jasmine tea that has steeped long enough to unfold its blossom in your mouth.

Soon the children will come up on the beach in their uniforms, red ties around their necks, blue blazers, white shirts: seated in an array on either side of a red trimmed, green rowboat. You walk up the bad road to town to buy a postcard, pass the child who loves to sing the English alphabet to you.

There is another wedding going on beyond the wall at the end of the block, bride in red and gold shawl, men in uniform. It is a celebration for something you know nothing about, except it seems that she will work hard, and her husband, that man drinking with his friends, may be gentle in nature, or may become flinty, hard, and like everywhere in the world, at every dawn, may raise his hand to her cheek. Yet he may not. Like everywhere in the world, he may cup her chin in his fingers, turn her face toward him with tenderness.

Who Are We to Say?

I want to let things be, let cab drivers tell me the fee without argument, hand the 35 rupees for a notebook to the woman draped in red and turquoise behind the counter without bickering. I do not know about the succession of her days, cannot say what is best for her as she sits among the shelves of handcrafted paper, watches me handle the bright pink notebook, stares as I turn over the pale green one. Perhaps she huddles around a fire with her sister before opening up the small room that is her store. She is born of a woman who also rose to Nepali dawn and before that a woman who might have lived farther up the hills on a farm where cows spiral along grassy trails.

From this distance: boarding school, the silverware lined up along the side of the plates in the sunlit mornings in the dining room, from those mornings I was raised up and sent into the world of New York weekends; from such noblesse, such easy life among window seats and leather chairs, from such ease of waking, who am I to say?

I am centered perhaps in whom I am not, as much as who I am. And I am not a bargain maker. I am not someone who wears her tall American whiteness with ease. If I could nurse a child, I would come with a heart full of practical gifts. If I could farm land in a way that grew crops to help blind children see, I might find a more permanent place here for a while.

Instead, with hands softened by books, pen and paper, I come as someone lost for the entire time I am here, looking for my reflection. I do not find mirrors reflecting me, but for now windows are enough: ways of taking in. I have no solution, not for the thick air in Katmandu, or the political situation in the far west of this mountainous country. I come here empty.

Who can say what is the way for a people to live their lives?

All I know is that if I wrote a letter to this country, I would bless its people, wish them well, ask them to continue to be gentle with the terraced hills, to treat women with great love and liberation and hold their children close, perhaps giving them pens, paper, books, and love all at once. This is, too, the same letter I would send home, to all who live in the hollers of Appalachia, the streets of Minneapolis, the broken and breaking hills outside of San Francisco. Raise up your daughters with grace and freedom, your sons with the same. Hold the elders in high regard, walk the streets, the mountain paths with grace.

Perhaps there are ways, then, to talk about living our lives, in Nepal, in the United States, midnight and noon the same moment as we lift our faces to the sky.

Here the journal ends.

I also found myself observing myself, while in Nepal. Maury hurt his leg while we were there and so I went into the foothills alone in the mornings. I wore a long skirt and boots as I had learned that women in pants were not respected. I found that I could actually move easier in a skirt and with tights on under the skirt the cold did not reach me on my climbs. One day I sat with a Yogi outside his ashram. We talked about subways in New York. He had visited the United States years ago.

The person I was in Nepal was more fearless than the one here. I am not sure why except that so much of life was lived outdoors and I felt very comfortable with that. When I returned I carried some of this new physical self with me.

Because I was struck by the poverty there, thin children, the cold water for washing even in the winter, the lack of electricity in the homes, I cannot be the same as I was when I first entered Nepal. And this difference is a good thing. It provides a way of standing off to the side of myself, watching how I speak. My mistakes are illuminated, my awkwardness apparent. Any impatience with broken English, any frustration when kids chatter with fellow Hmong or Latino or Somali friends in their native language seems ungenerous.

And add on the stories of these young people the aspect of escaping war or torture and it seems particularly cruel to penalize these children with impossible test measurements or impatience with language acquisition.

All my stereotypes of immigrant cultures have been demolished in these last years. I have worked with Somali girls whose heads are covered and who wear long skirts and who want to become lawyers. I had thought of Muslim women as relegated to the kitchen, the home.

I have worked with Hmong women who have run for Congress or started magazines or edited books. I have seen Latino, Hmong, and Somali women march with whites and African Americans for equal rights for workers. There is no end to my deeply buried assumptions, to what needs changing.

There are many who have written about the dislocation of being in another country than their country of birth. At the same time those in Nepal looked unlike me, unlike my family, we connected on some beginning level—laughter, children, tea. And what struck me on this trip, more than on any other journey I have taken in my life, is the abundance I have, as a white American woman, and the poverty of the country in which I was visiting. Even after I returned to the United States I felt uncomfortable, ill at ease for a while with my overstuffed grocery store, my nine-year-old Honda. And in contrast to this I remembered the generosity of those I met, offering to share tea with me or to bring me special food when I was ill.

The disorientation when surrounded by a language not my own was enough to convince me that those who come to the United States from other countries have strength and resilience I am not sure I could sustain myself. Combine this with coming here as a person of color—be it Somali or Hmong, Latino or Indian—and the achievement of immigrant students in learning the language, negotiating the school structure, understanding the maze of a new city is miraculous.

The whole time I was in Nepal—as beautiful as I believed it to be—I looked forward to eventually being *at home*. To believe I could never return to the land of my birth would have been unbearable. In all my time of depression or pain I have counted on having a place, a specific room, where I could hide, or celebrate, or escape. These rooms I inhabit are my safety, my center.

How many families who come from other places are struggling with post-traumatic stress disorder? How many students are living with mothers or fathers who feel this? How about the kids who have been relocated because of Katrina, or earthquakes or homelessness? To imagine not having a table that is familiar and a room that is predictable seems crucial in understanding students who arrive in our schools dislocated.

Reflection: What makes up a home for you? What is it like for you in a place surrounded by a language not familiar to you?

Suggestions: Learn certain phrases and greetings in the languages of your students. Post them over the door to your room: "Welcome," "Work Going On Here," "Artists Creating," "Scientists at Work." Explore community resources for translators during parent conferences or for child care or even a different place to meet your students. Make sure signage in the hallways is in the language(s) of those students who attend your school.

LESSON 43: SILENCE AND REFUGE

I moved to Washington Avenue North in 2002 as I was recovering from cancer surgery. We had finally made the break with our South Minneapolis neighborhood of thirty years, settling into a converted warehouse, just out of range of the most expensive and fashionable of the new developments, and thus affordable. It was September when we arrived. I needed months to find my energy, my desire to work. I was again, once the cancer was discovered, the lucky lady of decent income and health insurance. I had a fine surgeon and an amazing nurse who had me up and walking on the first day after the operation.

The thread of whiteness that connects my days is invisible. From Uncle Ed the head of pediatrics at Columbia University Hospital who helped me when Aaron was born and advised me on a decision involving treating him, to those who knew the best therapists and gynecologists, to the fine surgeon I had this last time, at age fifty-eight, I was connected. And I took full advantage of this knowledge. I am into my fifth year being cancer free.

The whole time I was in the hospital my body was held and pulled and rolled and handled by Rita and Marie, two black women, one from Liberia, one from Minneapolis. It seems to me that this kind of sacred work done with hands is negated. Yet it is what saves us.

After my surgery, I emerged into the world with a new appreciation for its beauty, for the fragile way even the most well-appointed of us live. I sit at our dining room table to write, in the mornings that I am free, and watch the sun slant across the wall of the building behind ours. Later the same wall will turn pink at sunset. If I sit on the stairs going up to a mezzanine bedroom I can see traffic on I-94 and can see the slowly rising new houses on the north side of Minneapolis.

Yesterday, I watched as a woman broke down reading a poem by Countee Cullen about being called a nigger when she was a child. The woman reading is a Ph.D., professor, and human rights worker. Yet in an instant, trying to get through Countee Cullen's words, she was taken back to her college years in Winona, Minnesota, when she made her first walk into town and was called this word three times before she got to her destination, a laundromat. She said, as she wiped her eyes, that she did not tell her own children, now grown, about this experience because they had enough to bear even now. And someone else said, "but these stories are important." And she answered, "I did not want to add to their hurt."

I wanted to jump in with a comparison, a similarity. I wanted to make the pain go away. I almost said this reminds me of Viet Nam veterans who never talked about what happened to them and some went crazy for not telling. Yet I did not speak. Some moments call for utter silence, for letting the story echo. Such silence may be the most powerful part of the telling, the receiving.

How often when I told friends or colleagues that I had cancer, would need surgery, they jumped in with stories of their own, their sisters, their mothers.

Yet the responses that were the most helpful were the ones that let the news sink in, that let it hang for a moment. They did not try to minimize. By comparing we are sometimes denying the unique quality of each experience of a disease or a hurt or a trauma. Each story of the Holocaust, each tale of suffering in a genocide, or at the hands of an abuser, is its own.

Later, we can go on, talk of similarities perhaps. Yet for that moment, the truth rests in the teller, in the way he or she has lived it.

How often do we let silence enter our classroom discussions? I know I rushed to call on the next student with his or her hand up, moved along to the next essay to be read aloud. I wish I had the respect for silence I have now. To let the stories rest, the statements echo, might have given students this gift of a silent moment before responding.

One of the times I found such quiet was when I taught writing and we wrote in our notebooks for ten minutes. The only real rule was quiet, a respect for each person's desire to write. I now wonder if students enjoyed this time as much for the dedicated moments free of noise, challenge, chatter as they did for the chance to create on the page.

In the years, since my book *A White Teacher Talks about Race* came out, I have traveled across the United States to talk with students, teachers, administrators of both private and public schools, colleges, police organizations, community groups, churches, and businesses about race, equity, and justice. I have taught in colleges—some private, some public universities. I come back to this room, this loft in the city. For the first time I feel truly at home in this part of the country. I am not sure if that is because I love being near Homewood Gallery across the bridge on Plymouth Avenue or if it is simply that I am in my sixties now and my lived history has settled in my body in a way that makes some sense. Or it may be that more than any house or apartment I have lived in, I have made this single space one that collects the colors I love, jazz photos, plants, paintings, books. I tend to think it is all of these things.

It helps to keep in mind that our classrooms can become refuges from the pressures, be it peer pressure on kids who are trying to succeed, or pressure on teachers who are speaking up about racism. It helps to know that some things are not complicated, do not require long hours pouring over dense research. Some things are simple and real: creating a space for all students to claim their voices and their stories, their skills and their aspirations; creating a space where students and teachers can go from there into the world of alliances and marches, advocacy and letter writing; creating a space where the painful interchanges can happen and can be recovered from, with compassion for each person in the room; creating a space where silence happens. This is what we can do.

I think of Elizabeth Alexander (2004) and her book of essays *The Black Interior*. She cites Gwendolyn Brooks's poem "Annie Allen," which includes descriptions of rooms. And then Alexander says: "She understands that any space can be sanctified, that space is what we have, and that if, as a poet she makes space visible, manifest, then she is getting us closer to the inner lives of her poetic characters who tell us so much about black people in a very specific place and time" (p. 16).

Reflection: How often does silence occur in your life? In your classroom? Do you believe most of your students feel safe in your classroom? What do you do to recognize the need for refuge: for yourself as well as for your students?

Suggestions: In every building there are teachers' rooms toward which students gravitate. Sometimes they even skip classes to go there. My son had an art teacher, John Kantor, who let Aaron come in and work on the wheel when he was having a rough day in school. He had to follow guidelines carefully to remain in the room. I have seen the toughest, most demanding and structured colleagues become the most popular. It is not a matter of getting away with anything that always attracts students. It may be the teachers' excitement about subject matter, their clear expectations, their ability to listen.

Put aside your defensiveness for a moment and explore what makes these teachers popular. Why do students sign up for their classes? Are there things you could take from what they do and apply them to your own classroom?

LESSON 44: RISK TAKERS

Recently I gave a talk at two schools that were part of a special interracial district, constructed to bring together inner-city students and suburban students from seven surrounding districts specifically to create integrated schools. I noticed that there were few teachers of color. Actually there was only one, and she taught in the elementary school. In the secondary school there were no teachers or administrators of color. In the blatant hierarchy of a racially segregated district, all of the educational assistants were black or Latino. I could not help but be concerned with what message this alone was sending to those students, both white and of color, who came together to learn in this district.

Following my September talk, I came back to meet with those who self-selected into a group who wanted to dig deeper into race and white privilege. In this group were many of the educational assistants, some white teachers, and an administrator—a white male. It was a rare experience for this group, as half of those present were of color. The administrator would barely participate, remained silent, even when I asked for responses from everyone. The rest spoke openly, and the conversation quickly came to a level I have witnessed in communities and meetings where those present are experienced in honest discussions of race. I was pleased, and as I learned the next day, so were a majority of the others, both black and white.

Soon after this meeting I got a note from another administrator. She wanted to know what was said, and who said it. I told her immediately that I could not tell her that. We had an unwritten contract that I believe is an assumed part the dynamics of this kind of meeting that calls for confidentiality. I did say that I was disturbed that the administrator who was there remained so silent, that this could have been intimidating and could have silenced others. They were a courageous group and his silence did not silence them. I also said that general areas of concern that came out of the meeting that needed to be addressed were discipline of kids of color compared to white kids, low expectations of black kids, and the lack of a truly multicultural curriculum in many classrooms. A few days after this, I learned that the male administrator had indeed gone to the principal of the secondary school and told her about the meeting. She proceeded to call in her teachers and assistants and scold them for saying negative things about the school in front of me, a visitor.

In whose interest, to whose benefit was this action? Was it to the benefit of the courageous teachers, the remarkable assistants who were willing to say what they saw and respond with great respect and honesty to the teachers? To the benefit of me? Was it to the benefit of students of color who felt isolated or unheard?

I think the only benefit derived from the suppression of such open, honest discussion was to the administrators who wanted to perpetuate the falsehood that they were running an educational system that truly addressed the needs of all their students and teachers.

Robert Colbert describes the role of the senior manager in the statement below. I believe it applies to the role of the principal in a school, or the superintendent in a school district:

> The best way to diminish this barrier [to diversity and inclusion] is to provide demonstrated commitment from senior managers regarding diversity and development initiatives. Accordingly, solid commitment must come in the form of recognition and rewards that improve an individual's position and status within the organization. Once a significant number of persons recognized as both "diverse" and "champions of diversity" are established within the organizational power structure, other managers will see little risk in associating with and promoting talented diverse candidates. (Designing Sustainable Diversity and Development Initiatives, 2005)

The schools that are making significant progress are those where principals put themselves on the line, supporting members of their staff and teaching force who are trying to address white privilege and diversity in an active way. These administrators work with their teachers to change the number of referrals of black males to special education, or find the most innovate ways to encourage students of color to take advanced classes, gifted programs.

I have also seen principals grant inordinate power to already empowered groups: to white parents who want their children in gifted programs in disproportionate numbers, to white teachers who want to continue to teach using a white male perspective. All the while courageous teachers—black, Latino, white, Asian, Native—are dangling in the wind as they propose changes, suggest more inclusive criteria for accepting students into advanced classes, and offer entirely new reading lists for all grade levels. All this time these teachers are the recipients of hostility from those who do not want to change.

The administrator is key in so many subtle ways in this struggle. We can only applaud the ones who are making the changes, who are bucking those on their faculty who dig in their heels. We can only hope we work for a principal like this one day.

Reflection: Are you encouraged to develop new curriculum and activities that address diversity and multiperspectives in your school? If not, are you isolated? How do you manage to do what you know is right, yet is not supported?

Suggestions: Meet with like-minded teachers, outside of school if you have to, to talk about things you want to change. Meet with those from other schools who are doing what you are doing. Find conferences and staff development opportunities that allow you to get the support you need.

LESSON 45: STUDENTS AS EXPERTS

When *White Teacher* came out and I did many readings and discussions around Minneapolis and St. Paul, I noticed the same young white man, sitting in the front row of the store, or library center or community auditorium where I was speaking, evening after evening. Finally, I went up to him, introduced myself and asked him what he was interested in, would he like to participate in one of the panels that often accompanied me? He said, no thanks, but he wondered if I would come and speak to his social studies class at South High, in Minneapolis. He read my book and he liked it and they were having talks in there and would I visit? It turned out I knew his teacher, had taught her in a graduate class a few years before. I agreed to get in touch with Tiffany.

A few weeks later I went to Joe's class. The group was a mixture of Somali, African American, white, Latino, and Native Americans, poor and rich, preppy and alternative. Because the teacher encouraged discussion, writing, and reading around issues of race and culture, they were very open. One young woman said, "My mother is Palestinian American, my father Somali, so I have so many mixtures. Do you call me black?"

Another young man said, "I am African American and I play the violin, and that surprises people cause I dress city, ghetto."

Finally Joe began to speak. He talked about playing soccer and sitting in locker rooms in suburban districts and hearing comments like,

"Man. I know my worst nightmare. It is ending up on the north side of Minneapolis! Whew! White man in that black world. Scary, man!"

Joe, his voice trembling, said it was hard to hear this, as his home was on the north side and they were talking about *his* neighborhood, one he loved. Because he was white, they assumed he must live in southwest Minneapolis. They did not know that South High took students from around the city into its magnet programs. So they spoke openly about how they felt about his section of the city. Racism affected him in a powerful way every week he played out of north Minneapolis. So many have stereotyped the north side they forget that 35 percent of the families in this part of town are white.

When Joe spoke, the rest of the class nodded their heads, the way kids often do when someone speaks from the heart, when even in that macho hormone-riddled time, a young man's voice trembles. There is great respect and kindness for those who speak the truth in classroom environments that encourage this. These rooms become communities, not any the less academically rigorous for it.

There is a scene in a recent book by Jonathan Kozol (2005) called *The Shame of the Nation* that makes clear how our students know much more about what is happening than we suspect or even than we ourselves know.

> Mireya, a high school student says, "I don't want to take hairdressing. I did not need sewing either. I knew how to sew. My mother is a seamstress in a factory. I'm trying to go to college. I don't need to sew to go to college. My mother sews. I hoped for something else."
>
> "What would you rather take?" I asked.
>
> "I wanted to take an AP class," she answered.
>
> Mireya's sudden tears elicited a strong reaction from one of the boys who had been silent up to now. A thin and dark eyed student, named Fortino, with long hair down to his shoulders was sitting on the left side of the classroom, he turned directly to Mireya.
>
> "Listen to me," he said. "The owners of the sewing factories need laborers. Correct?"
>
> "I guess they do," Mireya said.
>
> "It's not go'ng to be their own kids. Right?"
>
> "Why not?" another student asked.
>
> "So they can grow beyond themselves," Mireya answered quietly. "But we remain the same."
>
> "You're ghetto," said Fortino, "so we send you to the factory." He sat low in his desk chair, leaning on one elbow, his voice and dark eyes loaded with a cynical intelligence. "You're ghetto—so you sew!"
>
> "There are higher positions than these," said a student named Samantha.
>
> "You're ghetto," said Fortino unrelentingly to her. "So sew!" (p. 179)

To believe that these young people do not know what is expected or not expected for them is to give them little credit. They are perceptive. They take it all in.

As I come to a quieter time of my life, I feel even more the pull of *story*, the simple power of narration. I am convinced that daily listening and speaking is what will help us navigate the territory we inhabit together, with our multi-circuited and complex bodies, layered by memory. The "I want to tell you about yesterday . . ." impulse may be what will ultimately unite us.

I have heard more than once educators, preachers, teachers say something like the following: "I believe we need a listening revolution in this country." Not only does this strike me as profound and true but at the same time it strikes me that we are actually being *discouraged* from such a revolution, both in education and in our lives as a whole. We are rushed along by voices. We are rushed along by computers, by restrictive and regimented curriculum. In turn, we rush students along, too—to take the test, to accumulate the material, to absorb what we tell them. We are losing the chance to hear their stories, to let silence accumulate when necessary, to learn from what they tell us.

From the stories comes action. From thinking critically about what is written, shown on TV, or presented to them, come organized movements to change the very conditions of our students' lives. The more regimented we become, the more we lose students who are creative. It makes one wonder if this isn't the purpose of the regimentation itself—to keep us all in our places.

We can change this with the listening revolution, beginning in our classrooms. After all, while two bodies in the water swim in two separate worlds, they see similar blue landscape.

Epilogue

I still see that four-year-old girl on the porch in Dallas, realizing that her father did not understand the pain his word had caused the woman who cared for her. Later this girl will climb onto her father's lap for her story, let him carry her to bed, cover her with the blanket, and for a while slip into the ease of her world.

Years and years after this, she will remember her moment, the first day of her separation. As he holds her hand and dies an hour after she tells him to let go and the flowers he loved bow in the sun streaming into his room of blue walls and lace, she will mourn their separation, their inability to come together on some bridge they could never build.

In a few months, all five of my brothers and sisters will meet on Block Island, off Providence, Rhode Island. We will come with our own children and our grandchildren, and we will stand around the rented beach house with the wraparound porch and the view of the ocean. We will be reminded of those days at the Vineyard, of the odd times we came there after civil rights marches or jobs in settlement houses or years on the commune.

We will come as immigration lawyer from St. Paul, writer, teacher, and community activist from Minneapolis, Minnesota, builder of "green" houses from Asheville, North Carolina, sixth grade teacher and fantasy writer from Hot Springs, Arkansas, and computer troubleshooter from Stamford, Connecticut. Our children and their children may show up. I will also be there as a cancer survivor and a survivor of rape; Lesley survived melanoma, Claudia recently had hours of open-heart surgery. We will shop for groceries for vegans and meat eaters and the Zone dieters and chocolate fanatics and protein cravers and tea drinkers and those who cannot survive the morning without immediate coffee. Some will want to get to the beach and some will want to sit on the porch. Some will retreat to take a nap and some will talk until late into the night.

There is a kind of drifting we do when we are together, these sons and daughters of Boone and Susie, pilot and debutante, flyboy and dancer. All our lives our parents would bring us to places of water, salt, and wind. So when we can afford it, we meet by the ocean. We are orphans now and I think some of us feel a kind of liberation in this, along with yearning to be with our mother and father.

I cannot deny the life they gave me: it was full of a solid beauty, privilege, warmth, humor, and love. And too, it was governed by a New England straitlaced response, a tightening of the body. There is no way to erase the result of unearned privileges.

A white teacher in an urban school said to me a few days ago that what bothers him the most is that his black students cannot even seem to *imagine* themselves in college or in the college-oriented program in his predominantly black school. This never feels like a true possibility for them.

And even when I visit middle schools and high schools young African American men say to me that they do not see the purpose of setting goals for their future because they do not envision being alive in three or four years. This here, this lack of dreaming in their world is what we, with or without our privileges, our differences, must change.

Paolo Freire has said: "To speak a true word is to transform the world" (1970). It is in creating schools and classrooms that speak a true word, that challenge students and teachers, parents and administrators, secretaries and clerks to imagine what seems impossible, that we have a chance to transform the world.

Appendix A: Resources

PROFESSIONAL
Teaching Tolerance (magazine and website)
400 Washington Avenue
Montgomery, AL 36104
www.teachingtolerance.org

Rethinking Schools (journal and website)
Rethinking the Classroom (vol. 1, 2)
Reading, Writing, and Rising Up (guide to teaching writing)
1001 East Keefe Avenue
Milwaukee, WI 53212
www.rethinkingschools.org

Beyond Heroes and Holidays: A Practical Guide to K–12 Anti-Racist, Multicultural Education and Staff Development
Teaching for Change
PO Box 73038
Washington, DC 20056-3038
www.teachingforchange.org

Teaching for Change (catalogue)
K–12 Resources on Equity and Social Justice
www.teachingforchange.org

African American Registry (website)
www.aaregistry.com

EdChange (website)
www.edchange.org

GENERAL
"Why Are All the Black Kids Sitting at Separate Tables in the Cafeteria?":
    And Other Conversations about Race
Beverly Daniel Tatum

Braided Lives: An Anthology of Multicultural American Writing
Minnesota Humanities Commission, editor

Always Running: La Vida Loca, Gang Days in L.A.
Luis J. Rodriguez
Memoir

Makes Me Wanna Holler: A Young Black Man in America
Nathan McColl
Memoir

And Still We Rise: The Trials and Triumphs of Twelve Gifted Inner-City
    Students
Miles Corwin
Journalist account of a year at an inner-city Los Angeles school gifted
    program

Their Eyes Were Watching God
Zora Neale Hurston
Novel (high school)

Monkey Bridge
Lan Dao
Novel (high school)

Seedfolks
Paul Fleischman
Novel (middle school)

The Skin I'm In
Sharon G. Flake
Novel (middle school)

Coming of Age in America: A Multicultural Anthology
Mary Frosch, editor

Make Lemonade
Virginia Euwer Wolff
Novel

Unsettling America: An Anthology of Contemporary Multicultural Poetry
Maria Mazziotti Gillan and Jennifer Gillan, editors

That Kind of Sleep
Poems by Susan Atefat-Peckham

Appendix B:
Reflections and Suggestions

REFLECTIONS

In what ways was your early education difficult, jarring? In what ways was it in sync with your home culture?

What stories did your parents tell you?

What words did you learn or absorb that you used in school in your early years?

Did your vocabulary from home prepare you for school?

Did your teachers speak the way you spoke?

When were you told you were white, black, brown skinned?

When did you become aware you were part of a broader culture? How did your parents or relatives explain it to you?

How do you react to being called white if you are white, black if you are black?

What were you encouraged to do physically at a young age? What are your students encouraged to do?

Are there differences between your own children and your students in their expectations and instructions about safety?

How important was family to you growing up?

How important was it for you to do well as an individual in competition with others?

What did you do in groups?

Did you identify as part of any ethnic group? Geographical?

How separate is your life from those with a different skin color or from those of a different economic class?

What position did your parents have in relation to white people, people of color as you were growing up? What did you absorb from this? How has it played out in your teaching?

What status do people of color hold in your building compared to white people?

Did you often hear the word "white" to describe individuals? In the news? In your neighborhood or town?

Are you comfortable referring to yourself as white if you are white?

Try using this word "white" before each Caucasian person you refer to for one day in the way we often refer to the blackness or brownness of those who are not white. How does this feel? (See Thandeka's book *Learning to Be White* for a description of this challenge.)

Were there ever moments you sensed your upbringing about race was wrong? Hurtful?

Have you ever found yourself separating from your relatives or friends or colleagues over the topic of race?

How did you learn the meaning of racial epithets?

What were you expected to do in education as a child?

What was planned for you and when did you become aware of this?

Where did you get your hope?

How secure was your childhood?

Did you live in a secure and safe home while you were growing up? How has that influenced your world outlook? Your view of your students?

Do you feel guilt over your own advantages? Does it keep you silent or afraid to ask questions?

What do you know about now, that you were oblivious to as a child?

From whose perspective did you learn of current events, history, literature?

Do you assume students automatically respect you?

Were there times in your life when you did not automatically respect an elder?

How does it feel to be disrespected because of your skin color or have respect withheld?

What can you actually control in your classroom? What is out of your control?

What do you remember learning about your own race, religion, culture, or skin color? Can you create specific scenes or dialogue?

Make a list of all the ways your culture manifests itself in your life. How is gender treated in your religion? How are holidays celebrated? What rituals do you observe? Ask students to do this over the school year.

How did you learn about politics, the events of the news, as you were growing up?

From what point of view are history texts in your school written?

Do you live in an isolated enclave in terms of race or poverty? Is this a problem for you?

Have you always lived with those who are similar to you in terms of skin color? Religion? What are the advantages, disadvantages to this?

What stories and books do you remember from your childhood? What effect did this have on how you thought about the world?

Did you grow up with a lot of money? How did this affect you?

If you did not have money, what did you need from those around you?

What helped, what hindered you?

How would your life have been different if you had had money?

Write down a list of instructions you were given, either directly or indirectly, about behaving in the world.

Look up the headlines from some of the years you were an adolescent. What was going on then? What do you remember hearing about?

What were you allowed to do as an adolescent? Was it different from your brother? Your sister?

What were your frustrations between the ages of thirteen and eighteen?

What messages did you learn about race subconsciously as you got older and could read and argue and talk with your parents?

Think of a time when you did not act to stop teasing, racist jokes, words, or actions against certain people or a person. What did you learn from this? How has it influenced you?

Think of a time when you were an activist working for change. What motivated you? Where did it lead? Was it part of your church work? Neighborhood or community work?

When was a time you took your students outside the classroom?

When was a time you challenged tracking in your school?

What gives you hope in your school?

Do you have a different relationship with hope than your students or their families do? Articulate what that is, what might have made this difference.

What did you learn about the civil rights movement when you were in school? Growing up?

What did you learn about all that went on before the civil rights movement: the partition of Africa, slavery, Reconstruction, abolitionism?

When was a time you challenged prescribed curriculum? When you supported colleagues' demands for change? When you didn't?

In what ways have you been exposed to poverty? In working with students who live in poverty?

How has either wealth or financial stability affected your life?

How has poverty influenced you? Read the novel *Highwire Moon* by Susan Straight or the nonfiction book *Random Family* by Adrian Nicole LeBlanc to go deeper into the experience.

Have you ever been in a situation where you felt "other"? Did this surprise you?

Do you assume if you just explain, it will work out? Why do you think others may not feel this way?

Think of a time in your life when you were traumatized. What was your initial reaction? Did this change?

Think of a time when a student came to you with a story that was hard to hear. What did you do?

Have you ever had an experience of being truly immersed in a culture that was not the one you were raised in?

What part has luck or chance played in your teaching, in your life?

Why do you believe we stay in enclaves, live with those who look like us? Has there been a time in your life when you crossed this line?

Have you ever left a job, a school system in protest?

Has there ever been a time in your life when you lost your boundaries, your sense of yourself, and your family apart from your job? How did you cope with it?

What are some generalizations about poor students or students of color or students from certain cultural groups that you have been taught?

Has anyone taught you about white kids and how they behave generally?

Describe a time you were surprised to learn of your own success in reaching an unlikely student.

Where were you when Martin Luther King Jr. was shot? Were you alive? How old were you? Do you remember the effect this had on you?

What are advantages to integrated schools?

What are advantages to busing for integration?

What are advantages to separate academies? How do you reconcile the two?

What groups are you in that give you a sense of power? Does your church, athletic team do this?

In what context to do you feel in control, that you have real choices? Are these groups integrated?

Do you tend to equate gender and race prejudice?

As a woman, do you feel you have the same experiences as your black or white counterparts?

If you are male, do you feel gender affects the way you live? In what ways?

When did you learn to draw, paint, play music, perform in a play?

How important were these activities for you? How important are they for your students?

What is your teaching day like?

How much time do you have to read during the day? How much time to meet with other teachers?

How much time do you have to plan for the next day, or to grade papers?

How are people welcomed into your building? How are they viewed?

Where are you the most comfortable, city or suburb or rural area? How important is this in your teaching location?

What was your first year of teaching like? Your fifth? What did you learn in those years and afterwards?

Who do you refer to special education?

What group makes up the majority of special education students in your school? What categories are they referred in? Why do you think this is true?

Name some "moments of vision" in your life. What did they mean for you at the time? How did you change as a result of learning what you did?

How do you remain hopeful during times of despair?

What makes up a home for you?

What is it like for you in a place surrounded by a language not familiar to you?

How often does silence occur in your life? In your classroom?

Do you believe most of your students feel safe in your classroom?

What do you do to recognize the need for refuge: for yourself as well as for your students?

Are you encouraged to develop new curriculum and activities that address diversity and multiperspectives in your school? If not, are you isolated?

How do you manage to do what you know is right, yet is not supported?

SUGGESTIONS

Explore ways to create preschools where children spend part of their time with workers and teachers from their own culture.

Consider ways volunteers and community workers can come to school to be with young students from their earliest years.

Find songs that reflect cultures and languages and play them on a CD player each morning and afternoon as you work there.

Find heroes of all kinds. I have seen preschool teachers talk about heroes to kids as young as three years old, describing in simple terms their greatness, their accomplishments.

Use pictures books that are in Spanish or Hmong or Russian wherever possible, showing all students stories from many cultures and the similarities across these cultures.

Build in time for discussions of culture and even race at an early age.

Accept that your students may see you as "other" for a while.

Be patient.

Explore setting up a breakfast program if there is not one in your building.

Ask students themselves, perhaps in a questionnaire, about the places where they feel safe, where they don't feel safe.

Advocate for as much physically active time as possible for all students, no matter what grade you teach.

Create building-wide group projects.

In secondary schools, and even middle schools, organize students to survey the communities and neighborhoods to find out what the needs are, where there might be a garden planted, a small park created, a lot cleaned up.

Become comfortable with noise and activity as students work together. Have faith in them to get the job done while being social.

In the next month or two engage in all three categories of interaction that White and Cones speak about: conceptual, conversational, and experiential. Find ways to do this with a group of individuals you do not know well or are not necessarily comfortable with.

Develop exercises or find ones already created that work directly with prejudice. Have a conversation with your students about this. Who has to represent the whole group? Who is simply an individual? Is this fair?

Find allies in your work place who support your antiracism curricular concerns. Meet with them as often as you can.

Talk with colleagues, administrators about a clear understanding of how the school will deal with racial slurs and epithets.

Be ready to have conversations when events around race come up in the news.

From first grade on, work the idea of high school and beyond into the conversations in your classrooms. Imply that all your students will have choices about this.

Create chances for students to visit college campuses, to feel themselves physically *present* in a college environment.

Seek out teachers who are succeeding with kids you are having difficulty with. Often the expertise in working with students of all kinds is right in your building. Find time to observe these teachers.

If you have classes where students come and go within a year, try and tailor your instruction for them.

Create self-contained lessons so new students can jump right in.

Put together a packet that helps kids catch up when they come to your room.

Suggest someone start a student support group for students new to your school. This group can meet for five sessions, helping students adjust to their new environment.

Begin to ask your students, their parents, your colleagues about their lives, their hopes.

Survey students and parents each fall about what they want out of this year in your class in your specific subject.

Develop critical thinking skills in your students.

Create units, subjects, topics, themes from many perspectives.

Find materials that ask students, even young ones, to imagine and understand about perspectives not their own.

Talk about the principles of Kwanzaa at an all-white school, the Native American perspective on Columbus's arrival at a diverse middle school.

Offer a one-day-per-week, after-school, make-up time for students. Invite them into your room. This provides a time when they can talk with you about what is on their minds.

Build in time to build trust and community through initial exercises at the beginning of your course. It may seem difficult to take the time to do this at first, with so much material to cover, but ultimately it will pay off in fewer behavior problems and more cooperation among students.

Create a visceral, tactile, or active lesson for your students at least once a month.

Use interviewing as a way to understand literature, history or sociology, politics or immigration issues.

Use photographs, cooking, walking, and working on active projects to get students involved.

Take one event, in politics, history, literature, even science, and have students describe it from different points of view.

Pick an event: wedding, graduation, first day of school are examples. Have students randomly assigned to write about this even from different points of view: the bride, the best man, the ninth grade sister, and so on. Discuss why each might feel quite differently from another about what is happening. Allow humor to enter this activity.

Organize exchanges with schools around a similar assignment: reading the same novel and discussing it together.

Invite teachers from a school district unlike your own to develop a unit together in your subject area in secondary school or around a theme in elementary school.

Set up pen pal exchanges between students of color in different schools and arrange a final meeting or celebration after three months between the students.

Search the Internet, community centers, and libraries for stories and literature that present complexity, intelligence of characters of many kinds of cultures, races, and economic levels.

Ask students to write their own narratives and stories as often as you can, even in history class. For example, ask them to imagine the story of a young boy or girl in a certain era.

Use the power of story as a way in—to literature, history, science, psychology.

Think of ways to make it possible for poor kids to learn: computer access, after-school homework hours, breakfast programs, supplies for students who don't have them, cell phones for homeless families. Become an advocate for one of these ideas.

Ask students to list instructions they have been given by their parents, guardians, church group, peers. Discuss these in class and compare your list to those of your students.

In every way possible try to create families or houses or learning communities that provide small groups for adolescent students.

Give students time to ask questions, argue, explain their viewpoint.

Become comfortable when the topic of race comes up. This is where they need to feel they can try it out.

Ask someone to tape a class you are having difficulty with. Watch it with a friend, mentor, coach. Look for subconscious messages you are sending to students through tone of voice, body language.

Organize cross-age tutoring, class-to-class escort services, and student leadership teams that will influence seventh, eighth, or ninth graders at a crucial time in their development.

Use peers to influence peers, trying to be sensitive to how this will seem, and develop ways to counter negativism.

Brainstorm with colleagues what a supportive, hip school might be like.

Conduct a survey of needs, issues, or concerns among your students and their parents. Brainstorm projects with them after you look at the results of the surveys. What might you focus on?

Help students become realistic. Combine this with research, writing, and artistic subjects for credit.

Organize a continuing dialogue with colleagues and students about institutional racism, perpetuation of privilege, and how to break this pattern. Assume it will be uncomfortable and will take time.

How can you literally and physically extend school into the community?

Could parents take classes at your high school for their GED?

Could you set up an evening tutoring service for parents who are English Language Learners (ELL)?

Create a text that is an alternative to your assigned book.

Use the regular text as a way for students to explore what is *not* included.

Look over the sidebar in chapter 5 that outlines suggestions for working with students in poverty. How is your building doing in this regard?

Brainstorm ways of forming coalitions with the community from which your school comes, or with city or state groups—be they working for fair labor and housing, in support of cultural events or libraries, or voting efforts. Choose one area in which to expand your involvement.

Explore ways for students to form coalitions with each other.

Include parents whenever possible in the selection of teachers and principals.

Create site councils, PTAs, opportunities for parents, white and black, to get together (in separate groups if they feel this is necessary at times) at regular intervals.

Create a woman's book group, discussion group.

Explore same sex math classes.

Brainstorm ways to reach both young men and young women in order to break cycles of failure or lack of confidence.

When a new immigrant group moves into your school district, explore with city and state workers what those students will need when they arrive at your school door. Find articles for all teachers and staff to read about this group, keeping in mind the danger of stereotyping or limiting expectations.

Create a school theme, lesson plan, or a unit topic around the idea of Insiders and Outsiders. Bring in historical examples of those inside and outside the system who worked for change.

Create a class character with your students. Encourage them to imagine this character's likes and dislikes, background, job, house. Continue by having them describe this character in different situations. Encourage them to make her do unexpected things, unusual things given her race or culture.

Form a support group for new teachers in your building.

Become an unofficial mentor for a new teacher whom you admire and want to help navigate the profession.

Create new and original ways to recognize King's birthday.

Think about reconciliation hearings, art projects, murals, action learning units.

Work on activist solutions with students as early as grade four to change what Dr. King would have wanted changed.

Think of ways within your school system to create oases of support and safety for cultural groups. These could include once-a-week meetings, half days of immersion in their culture, whole days in separate settings with exchanges built in. What would fit your district?

Figure out how to create a network of support groups for students of all kinds.

Design your classes in ways to give students a chance to feel a sense of control of their education: contracts for grades, choice of literature or projects.

Set up a faculty and staff women's support group with women of color included from the beginning. Begin the sometimes uncomfortable discussions about race together.

Think of ways to combine courses into interdisciplinary combinations: music and math, home economics and chemistry, literature and social studies, shop and sociology. Think of combinations you would not ordinarily put together and imagine how it might be done.

Find ways to read or draw or daydream.

Skip the lounge. Turn off the lights in your classroom during lunch.

Talk with others about how to achieve some time to work.

Stay one hour later if you can in order to bring less work home on as many days as possible.

Consult those who work as attendance clerks, hall monitors, secretaries about a child you are concerned about.

Help set up discussions and training sessions for all staff and teachers. Make this part of the negotiations for different unions in your district.

Watch for new teachers in your building. Ask them out for coffee once in a while.

Create a small community of like-minded teachers in your building and meet as often as you can. Include new teachers in this group.

Review the sidebar in chapter 8.

Consider changing the situation of overreferral. How can your school address this, given these factors?

Take a "mental health" day. Do something you love unconnected to school. Go to a movie, draw, take a yoga class in the middle of the day.

Learn certain phrases and greetings in the languages of your students. Post them over the door to your room: "Welcome," "Work Going on Here," "Artists Creating," "Scientists at Work."

Explore community resources for translators during parent conferences, or for child care or even a different place to meet your students.

In every building there are teacher's rooms toward which students gravitate. Sometimes they even skip classes to go there. My son had an art teacher, John Kantor, who let Aaron come in and work on the wheel when he was having a rough day in school. He had to follow guidelines carefully to remain in the room. I have seen the toughest, most demanding and structured colleagues become the most popular. It is not a matter of getting away with anything that always attracts students. It may be the teachers' excitement about subject matter, their clear expectations, their ability to listen.

Put aside your defensiveness for a moment and explore what makes these teachers popular. Why do students sign up for their classes? Are there things you could take from what they do and apply them to your own classroom?

Meet with like-minded teachers, outside of school if you have to, to talk about things you want to change.

Meet with those from other schools who are doing what you are doing.

Find conferences and staff development opportunities that allow you to get the support you need.

References

Alexander, Elizabeth (2004). *The Black Interior*. Minneapolis: Gray Wolf Press.

Colbert, Robert (2005). *Designing Sustainable Diversity and Development Initiatives*. Manuscript.

Dalton, Harlon (1995). *Racial Healing*. New York: Doubleday.

Delpit, Lisa, and Joanne Kilgour Dowdy, eds. (2001). *The Skin That We Speak: Thoughts on Language and Culture in the Classroom*. New York: New Press.

DuBois, W. E. B. (1903). *The Souls of Black Folk*. Available at Google Books, 181.

Freire, Paolo (1970). *Pedagogy of the Oppressed*. New York: Continuum Press.

Hull, Gloria T., Patricia Bell Scott, and Barbara Smith, eds. (1982). *But Some of Us Are Brave*. New York: Feminist Press.

Hurston, Zora Neale (1937). *Their Eyes Were Watching God*. New York: Harper and Row.

Koerner Report. (1992). Cited in *People's Chronology*, James Treger. New York: Henry Holt.

Kozol, Jonathan (2005). *The Shame of the Nation: the Restoration of Apartheid Schooling in America*. New York: Crown Publishers.

LeBlanc, Adrian Nicole (2004). *Random Family: Love, Drugs, Trouble, and Coming of Age in the Bronx*. New York: Scribner.

Loewen, James T. (1995). *Lies My Teacher Told Me.* New York: Touchstone.

Maslow, Abraham (1943). "A Theory of Human Motivation," *Psychological Review* 50: 370–396.

McIntosh, Peggy (1988). "White Privilege: Unpacking the Invisible Knapsack," excerpted from Working Paper 189, "White Privilege and Male Privilege: A Personal Account of Coming to See Correspondences through Work in Women's Studies." Wellesley College Center for the Research on Women, Wellesley College.

Milner, H. Richard, and Tyrone Howard (2004). "Black Teachers, Black Students, Black Communities, and Brown: Perspectives and Insights from Experts," *Journal of Negro Education,* Summer.

Peterz, Kimberly Suzette (1999). "The Overrepresentation of Black Students in Special Education Classrooms," *In Motion Magazine,* at www.inmotionmagazine.com.

Powell, Kevin (2003). *Who's Gonna Take the Weight: Manhood, Race, and Power in America.* New York: Three Rivers Press.

Powers, Richard (2004). *The Time of Our Singing.* New York: Picador.

Silko, Leslie Marmon (1977). *Ceremony.* New York: Penguin.

Straight, Susan (2002). *Highwire Moon.* New York: Anchor.

Thandeka (1999). *Learning to Be White.* New York: Continuum Publishing.

White, Joseph, and James Henry Cones, III (1999). *Black Man Emerging: Facing the Past and Seizing a Future in America.* New York: W.H. Freeman.

Woolf, Virginia (1953). *A Writer's Diary.* New York: Harcourt Brace Jovanovich.

Zinn, Howard (1980). *A People's History of the United States.* New York: Harper Collins.

Index

About the Author

Julie Landsman taught in Minneapolis public schools for twenty-eight years. She has recently taught at Carleton College, Northfield, Minnesota, and has been an adjunct professor at Hamline University as well as the University of St. Thomas, both in St. Paul. Her books *Basic Needs: A Year with Street Kids in a City School*, and *A White Teacher Talks about Race* are memoirs about her days in Minneapolis public schools. *White Teacher* is in its second printing. She coedited a book with Professor Chance Lewis from Texas A&M University titled *White Teachers in Diverse Classrooms: Creating Community, Combating Racism* released in April 2006. This book is already in its second printing. She and Chance have led numerous workshops throughout the country and have completed a DVD to accompany their text. She has edited two books for young people: *From Darkness to Light*, and *Welcome to Your Life*, with David Haynes. *Diversity Days*, a book of activities for teachers to help them create a community of voices in their classrooms is another of Landsman's books for teachers. Her *Tips for Creating a Manageable Classroom* is used for many new teachers in both St. Paul and Minneapolis school districts as well as others in the United States. She recently won a Loft Literary Center Career Grant, which she used to give talks in various schools and literary centers in New York. Her poem "Laos on the Radio" appeared in the February 2004 issue of *Paj Ntaub*, a magazine centering on Hmong experience and culture. Her short story "Suspension" recently won the New Letters Award in Fiction. She also collaborated on a poetry/image project with photographer Bill Cottman. Julie Landsman has been a featured speaker on white privilege in many venues, including Bangkok, Thailand, in March 2006 at a conference for the Near East South Asian schools association. She is a frequent contributor to *Educational Leadership* magazine. Landsman is also working with Homewood Gallery on a storytelling/photography project centered on the women of north Minneapolis and the stories they have to tell. She lives in Minneapolis with her husband, Maury.